Feel Good About Selling

Increase Your Sales
Keep Your Integrity

Ted Olson

© Copyright 2022 Ted Olson

ISBN - 978-0-9885352-7-5

Feel Good About Selling - Increase Your Sales. Keep Your Integrity.

All rights reserved. No part of this book may be reproduced or transmitted in any form or by any means, electronic or mechanical, including photocopying, recording, or by any information storage and retrieval system without the prior written permission of the author, except for the inclusion of brief quotations in critical reviews and other non-commercial uses permitted by copyright law. For permission requests, contact the author.

Village Viewpoint, LLC
FeelGoodAboutSelling.com
6 Beatrice Ln.
Medway, MA, 02053

Contents:

Acknowledgements   4

Introduction   5

Part One: Rethinking Sales

Chapter 1: Reasons You May Not Feel Good About Selling   9

Chapter 2: A Different Way to Think About Sales   15

Chapter 3: Your Unique Role in the Sales Journey   20

Chapter 4: A Different Kind of Sales Approach   23

Part Two: Positioning You to Stand Out

Chapter 5: Your Public Service Announcement   32

Chapter 6: The Power of Contrast   40

Chapter 7: The Power of Reframe   49

Chapter 8: Helping You Stand Out   58

Part Three: Exploring Need In A Safe Environment

Chapter 9: How To Have Great Sales Conversations   69

Chapter 10: Creating A Safe Environment — 100

Part Four: Presenting For Ownership

Chapter 11: How to Present a Solution So That Your Prospect Owns It — 108

Chapter 12: Helping Your Prospect Get to the Finish Line — 126

Part Five: Applying Sales Principles In Your Context

Chapter 13: How You Can Put It All Together — 134

Chapter 14: Handling the Three Most Common Objections — 138

Chapter 15: Pre-call Planning That Helps You Help Your Prospect — 154

Chapter 16: Principles That Will Help You Feel Good About Selling — 160

Taking Your Sales To The Next Level — 164

Appendix: Downloadable Sales Guides — 165

References: Notes, Nods & Citations — 166

Acknowledgements

I need to start by thanking my wife who helped me turn two book ideas into one great book idea. Thanks to the sales leaders that have molded and shaped me over the years: Denise Olson (Yes, my mom), Mike Shaloub, Jason Miner, David Helgeson, Drew Fortin, Lee Pichette, and Matt Poepsel. I want to call special attention to one of my sales mentors, Jim Speredelozzi. He filled some gaps and catapulted my sales skills to new heights. Without Jim, this book would not have been possible. Thank you! And super special thanks to the prospects and clients, the sales people, the sales teams, and the business owners, consultants, and entrepreneurs who have put up with me.

Introduction

It's hard to feel good about selling when so much of sales is off-putting. Like many, you may be filled with ambiguity, reluctance, or even anxiety when it comes to sales. Perhaps you need to sell to run your business. Maybe you're a consultant, a small business owner, or an entrepreneur. You may be in a sales role and you're feeling uncomfortable. Maybe you've felt uncomfortable for a long time.

I get it.

I've been there.

I want you to feel good about selling. I want you to be successful. That's the goal of this book.

Whatever your reasons, this book will empower you not only to sell, but to sell differently and to feel good about it. In the chapters ahead, you'll unpack a step-by-step approach that reframes sales and empowers you to sell in a way that resonates with you. You'll also learn to avoid bad sales habits that irritate your customers and hurt your sales efforts.

Rather than traditional approaches that use pressure tactics and manipulation, this book will show you how to help others honestly and with authenticity. You'll know the words to say and have the confidence to say them. You'll feel good about selling. If you're skeptical, that's good. I ask one thing - keep an open mind. What follows isn't for everyone. But if you have the courage to think differently and practice some simple principles, you're already on your way.

Sales tactics don't feel good for anyone. Including you. Yet most sales training methodologies are filled with manipulative high pressure tactics.

This is bad for you and bad business. It hurts your brand. It costs you sales. It upsets your customers.

This is nuts!

I want you, or you and your sales team, to be able to help make people's lives better and not offend or put off your customers.

Here's the new reality:

Business has changed - drastically. We live in a new era.

Buyers have grown weary of outdated sales tactics, high pressure, and manipulation.

Sellers who embrace this change will win. Those who don't will flatline and ultimately fade away.

The old way of sales = combative, high pressure, manipulation, and rigid sales approaches.

The new way of sales = relationships, guidance, education, a safe environment of invitation, choice, and flexibility.

Buyers have high expectations. Meeting them requires new ways of thinking about sales.

***

This book is broken into five parts with sixteen chapters. It has been written to be read straight through in order, but feel free to jump around and use it as a resource.

PART ONE
RETHINKING SALES

CHAPTER 1

Reasons You May Not Feel Good About Selling

Sales has a bad reputation for sure. The stereotypical used-car salesperson often comes to mind. You can picture the greasy hair, the manipulative smile, and the shirt collar that's way too big. Or, perhaps the aggressive sales tactics depicted in the 1992 film, *Glengarry Glen Ross* put it over the top for you. The pressure to *always be closing* didn't sit right in your soul. But there's something else - something more fundamental. Your feelings about sales can likely be traced to a contrast with your core values. When sales is depicted as pressuring, pushing, or manipulating people, you immediately recognize that's not who you are. The technical term for this is cognitive dissonance. That is, you are not comfortable doing things that are at odds with who you are. It's no wonder selling may not feel great.

I don't blame you.

You would never want those stereotypical things to be associated with you and who you are as a human being. So it makes a lot of sense that you'd be reluctant to engage in anything like that.

This is a good thing.

This tension is telling you that you care about being honest, truthful, and helpful. These are good things in sales, but they're often absent. You'll see how to unpack them in the chapters ahead. Following are some other issues that get in the way of sales feeling good. This is not an exhaustive list, but these seven cover a lot of ground.

Inauthentic

There's a stereotype that salespeople are supposed to be super social, talkative, and friendly. While these *can* be positive attributes, they can also be off-putting. Think about it: don't you hate it when a salesperson won't shut up? They just keep talking as if the more they talk the more you'll be willing to buy. Or, they have no personal boundaries, and they act like you're their new best friend. It comes off as superficial and annoying. I remember a time when I was buying a car and the salesperson started asking about my family, my work, and my hobbies. I knew he was trying to build rapport, but it was uncomfortable and poorly done. He crossed my personal boundaries. These characteristics and actions likely go against what you deem to be acceptable behavior.

Sales Skills

Another reason selling may not feel good is that you think you don't have the skills. You could never "pitch" someone. Perhaps you stumble over your words, your mouth dries up, or your heart pounds right out of your chest. Maybe it's all of the above! You see others who seem to sell so naturally and think, "I could never do that." If this is you, you're a lot closer to being able to sell really well than you may think. The core principles and approach laid out in this book will equip you with the skills to sell like a pro and feel good about it.

Introverts

Being an introvert is another reason sales may not be your cup of tea. Because of this, you're not comfortable with presentations or being the center of attention. You don't like putting yourself out there. To you, it would seem like showing off, or being too pushy or assertive. It's just too much. You may indeed be an introvert, or shy, or uncomfortable, and it may be overwhelming to you right now. The good news is that the approach in this book will show you that you don't have to be something you're not. Instead, you will tap into your existing strengths and use some new tools and ideas to empower you.

High Pressure

Perhaps you are someone who just doesn't like the pressure of sales. Having your paycheck depend on your results can be uncomfortable. In sales you are literally measured by your performance. It can make you feel quite vulnerable. Sales can be like living in a pressure cooker. It's great when the temperature is just right, but it's often too hot or too cold. These extremes can be unpleasant. This, combined with quotas, long hours, and the stress, is enough to turn you away. It's just too risky. The good news is that it doesn't have to be this way.

Tainted By Association

You may be wary of being tainted by association. To get an idea of what this might feel like, glance at some popular sales books that exude bravado or even toxic masculinity.

- *Way of the Wolf*. Umm, do I have to behave like an animal?

- *Sell or be Sold*. Is there some sort of battle going on between me and my prospect that I'm not aware of?

- *Fanatical Prospecting*. Can't I just do some *regular* prospecting?

- *Ninja Selling*. Do I have to hurt people? And doesn't this border on cultural appropriation?

- *The Secrets of Closing the Sale*. Do I need to join some sort of secret society?

To be fair, I've not read all of these books, and I'm using humor to make a point. However, the tone and approach suggested in these titles may make you steer clear of the sales crowd.

Bad Experiences

Another reason sales may be distasteful to you is that you've had bad experiences with salespeople. You've felt the pressure. You've felt like you were being cornered. It made you uneasy. You may have politely (or abruptly) stopped the conversation and walked away. I once had a salesperson literally ask me to show him cash in my wallet to prove that I was committed to buying. I've had sales people call me repeatedly, first on my cell, then on my business line. They flood my email and ping me on LinkedIn, talking about how great they are and asking for 15 minutes of my time. They want to send me a gift or buy me a coffee just to get on my calendar. The annoyance and emotional toll of these experiences have a long shelf life. You would never want to treat people this way, and you wouldn't want people to feel the way you felt.

Rejection

Finally, there's the classic fear of rejection. No one likes this. It's uncomfortable. It makes you feel vulnerable, exposed, and unworthy. To put yourself in the position of receiving a no - especially when it's something you are passionate about - is a jab at the very core of your being. Like George McFly in *Back to the Future*, you declare, "I just don't think I can take that kind of rejection." Not being super-excited about sales in this light is normal. It's simple self-preservation. It's totally understandable.

Again, this is not an exhaustive list of all the reasons why sales might not be your jam. Perhaps some have resonated more than others.

Fair warning: not everything in this book will resonate with you. However, if you're open to a different approach, you may be pleasantly surprised. Sales - good sales - is very different from these stereotypes.

Here's something that you may find interesting: roughly 50% of all the salespeople I train tell me that they are anxious and/or uncomfortable with sales. Some have stated that they see selling as a necessary evil they have to endure. Others are plagued or even paralyzed by fear. Here's another fun fact: the 50% of the salespeople who say they like sales aren't very good at it. They have so many bad habits it's painful to listen to them talk with prospects. They have to unlearn ingrained habits and build new ones. So don't feel bad if you don't like sales, or if you're anxious, or uncomfortable, or even if you feel like you lack the skill set. You are not alone. What's ahead will provide you a fresh lens on selling and how you can excel in your context.

CHAPTER 2

A Different Way to Think About Sales

When I ask people to define sales, I get a wide variety of responses. Here are a few:

- Sales is a transaction
- It's providing a solution
- Sales is solving a problem
- It's an exchange of value
- Sales is transferring excitement
- It's about building trust and relationships
- Sales uncovers pain and fixes it

These definitions are not wrong. They're just incomplete. The dictionary definition of sales does not help much either. It defines sales as an exchange of a commodity for money. There's more to selling than that!

The following one-sentence definition is a more complete picture of what sales really is and offers a different way to think about sales. It will be the working definition for this book.

Sales is the process of helping someone make a positive change and allowing them to own it.

A bit different, right? You don't typically hear *sales* and *helping someone* in the same sentence. Within this short definition are six principles that are missing from many sales methodologies.

Principle #1 - Sales is a process

Sales is a process of varying lengths of time and steps. There are many opinions on what this should look like. What's clear, however, is that sales is about movement. It's often described as a single-point-in-time-transaction. It's not. A transaction certainly does occur at some point, but a process has taken place first. Put another way, sales is a journey where an individual or organization is seeking to move from one point to another. This journey may happen in one conversation or over the course of months or even years, but it's a journey the buyer is on and understanding your role in this makes all the difference. Helping people on a journey is a good thing.

Principle #2 - Sales is about helping people

Helping people is a core mindset in this book. Without it, sales becomes a means to an end for the sales person (e.g., money, prestige, power, control). These things are not necessarily bad.

Making them the end is. The goal in sales is to help people. Most agree manipulating people is bad. Everyone agrees that helping people is good. Yet, as we explored in chapter one, many hate sales, the profession, and even salespeople. This disconnect illustrates the point that too often and for too long salespeople have failed to focus on helping people. Sales is not about manipulating people. It's not about tricking them. And it's not about cheating anyone. Sales is about you helping your prospect to get to where they want to go.

Principle #3 - Sales involves making a positive change

Sales is about making things better for your prospect. Helping people requires guiding them to move in a positive direction. You want to help an individual or an organization move toward something better: a better situation, less pain, more freedom, etc. In a very real sense, sales is about leadership. You are helping people move forward from one position to a better position. Good sales helps your prospect to envision and take hold of something better. While change can be scary for a prospect, good sales helps to remove risk to ensure the buyer's success. Unfortunately, many salespeople love to be the hero. They want to see themselves as the closer, the rainmaker, the person who gets it done. If this is you, you may want to throw this book out. I will not be making you the hero. Sales is about making your prospect the hero. You are simply a guide throughout the journey.

Principle #4 - Sales involves solving problems

When you're helping someone make a positive change it can be a painful journey for them. Your prospects' journey will be fraught with challenges to varying degrees. They can appear in many forms. They may be emotional, financial, or both. For example, your prospect may be seeking lawn care to escape the embarrassment of a messy yard, or to save time, or to avoid the pain of doing it themselves. Or perhaps your services are required to help an organization rebrand itself. In this example, the company could be wrestling with the pain of lost revenue, toxic culture, poor leadership, or lost market share. Your buyers are always dealing with some kind of problem. Understanding your buyer's problem and what matters most to them is key to helping them on their way. Sales is a problem-solving profession.

Principle #5 - Sales means allowing the prospect to take ownership

This is the most confusing principle in sales. This process/journey - this movement from one place to another - is something the prospect needs to own. **They** need to make the decision for positive change. You are all too familiar with pressure tactics and cajoling. This is because many salespeople believe they own this decision so they push and manipulate and control. This is likely one of the reasons sales is off-putting to you. The good news is that a salesperson's job is not to sell. A salesperson's job is to help someone solve a problem, and to help them take ownership of solving that problem. This changes everything.

Principle #6 - Sales is a relationship

You can't ignore the relational nature of this journey. The prospect is the hero of the story. You are the guide (more about this shortly). Of course, there are antagonists. These are the dragons that our prospects need to slay. When you understand your part in the relationship, it removes unnecessary pressure from you. Your prospect will feel better too. And it helps you avoid a lot of the things you probably don't like about sales anyway. Sales is a human-first endeavor.

***

As you can see, this new definition of sales and the principles embedded within it changes things quite a bit. Without these principles, your customers face annoying sales techniques. They have to endure aggressive behaviors. They are not treated with the dignity and respect they deserve. If you're open to it, the chapters ahead can help you to become that trusted individual that clients and prospects will seek out.

> **Sales is the process of helping someone make a positive change and allowing them to own it.**

Chapter 3

Your Unique Role in the Sales Journey

Before looking at a different kind of sales approach, it's important to clarify your role in the sales journey. In the past, you have been taught, or have witnessed, sales approaches that cast the salesperson as the star in the show. The salesperson is typically seen as charismatic, engaging, and always knows exactly what to say. They're the center of attention. The star. However, when the salesperson is the star, it confuses the prospect. Why? Because the prospect is supposed to be the star of the show. The prospect is supposed to be the hero. The prospect is the one who needs to overcome their obstacles.

This idea is often referred to as the hero's journey thanks to Joseph Cambell's book, *The Hero's Journey*. In sales, this translates to helping customers (heroes) solve problems. This is an old but very relevant idea. Dale Carnegie wrote in 1936: "...if salespeople can show us how their services or merchandise will help us solve our problems, they don't need to sell us. We'll buy." Zig Zigler touches on this with his famous quote, "You can get everything in life you want if you will just help enough other people get what they want." Making heroes is also embedded in the practice of servant leadership. For a couple easy reads on the hero's journey, check out Donald Miller's book, *The Making of a Story Brand* and Nancy Duarte's book, *Resonate*.

To feel good about selling you need to become a hero-maker. You need to be the guide on a prospect's journey to help them fight the good fight. The guide is critical to the journey. In most great movies there is a hero, a guide, and a nemesis. Look for these the next time you're watching a movie. Luke in *Star Wars* needed to battle the forces of the dark side. He needed to take out the death star. He even had to battle his own father. Who helped Luke? His guides - Obi Wan and Yoda. In *The Karate Kid*, Mr. Miyagi was the guide who helped the hero (Daniel) slay the dragons of Cobra Kai. Katniss had Haymitch in The Hunger Games. These guides felt a sense of pride and purpose in helping their heroes find their way. Being the guide, not the hero, feels so much better.

The key point for you is that **the guide bears great responsibility**. The guide seeks to do good and treats people with dignity. The guide helps heroes see things differently, but allows the hero to make the choice for themselves. It's what makes great movies. It's also what makes selling feel good. When you help your prospects slay their dragons it feels good for you and your prospects.

One of the biggest mistakes sales professionals make is misunderstanding their role. They cast themselves as the hero. They seem to go out of their way on websites and social media to portray themselves as the superstar. A quick glance at some LinkedIn profiles illustrates this. Some of the common statements include things like: changemaker, energizer, and/or revenue multiplier. The salesperson who highlights their achievements risks confusing their prospects and missing out on sales.

To be clear, this doesn't mean you don't possess expertise (Obi Wan, Yoda, and Mr. Miyagi certainly did). It means that if you put your expertise into the service of others, you'll be a hero-maker. I hope the idea of being someone who helps people overcome their obstacles sits a little better with you. I hope it makes you feel good. If it does, the approach ahead may be just what you've been looking for.

Chapter 4

A Different Kind of Sales Approach

You've likely experienced and/or used any number of sales systems throughout your career. As a customer, perhaps you felt like you were being cornered. Or, maybe you felt pressure to make a decision on the spot and you weren't ready. The feelings you experienced during these interactions resulted from sales approaches designed to get to a close. Depending on the context (and the salesperson), some work better than others. As a salesperson, you may have been instructed in some of these pressure techniques and directed to use them in your sales context. You may have even mastered a particular approach. The good news is that you're going to learn a different approach to help people make a positive change and allow them to take responsibility for the close.

To be fair, some sales systems are really good. If they're adopted, practiced, and adapted to the context, they can produce quite predictable outcomes. That said, these sales systems are often multi-step sales processes that can confuse both the salesperson and the prospect. Buyers rarely follow a salesperson's system; in spite of the fact that sellers spend an inordinate amount of time and energy trying to lasso their prospects to follow it. This creates a battle in the wrong place: between you and your prospect. Miller notes that the fight should not be between the hero (your prospect) and the guide (you). The fight is between the hero and the antagonist (the problem they're experiencing). The sales approach ahead can be imagined as the journey you need to take with your prospect as they prepare to do battle.

Unlike long or complicated sales methodologies, there are only three movements to this sales process. I'll unpack these in more depth as we go, but these are the three movements.

Movement One: Positioning

What? Positioning? What about prospecting? Yes, this veers away from traditional sales. Why? You can't prospect well until you know how to position yourself well. Get positioning right and prospecting becomes much easier. We'll cover this in depth together. For now, this movement is about positioning you in such a way as to gain your prospect's interest. You want to get their attention and you want to get them interested in working with you. This is a movement from Attention to Interest. It's the idea of helping your prospect be interested in what you have to offer.

Movement Two: Exploring

Exploring seeks to understand if and how you can help your prospect. Now that you have their attention and interest, exploring uncovers what really matters to your prospect and how you can best help. The exploring movement is a move from Interest to Buy-in. That is, your prospect sees you as a potential solution to their problem.

Movement Three: Presenting

Presenting is the movement in which your prospect takes ownership to purchase your product and/or services. This is the move from Buy-in to Ownership. This is where your prospect is saying, "Yes, I want to work with you; let's do this."

The acronym for this is PEP - Positioning, Exploring, and Presenting.

MOVEMENT ONE **POSITIONING**	MOVEMENT TWO **EXPLORING**	MOVEMENT THREE **PRESENTING**
Attention → Interest Positioning you to gain a prospect's interest	**Interest → Buy-In** Exploring if and how you can help your prospect	**Buy-in → Ownership** Presenting a solution for prospect ownership

You can think about this sales approach in terms of a movie. Positioning is the movie trailer. Exploring is the story. Presenting is like the climax and resolution of the story.

If you've ever watched a movie trailer and said, "That looks interesting, I want to see that," that's the movement from getting someone's attention to getting them interested. It's the movement from Attention to Interest. That's positioning.

As you watch the movie, you are engrossed in it - whether it's the excitement or the drama or both. It doesn't matter how early you have to get up the next day, you're staying up to watch it. You are bought in. That's the movement from Interest to Buy-in. That's exploring. This is often called discovery, or exploring need. I call it exploring as it helps to remind me to stay open and curious.

Movement three is the climax and resolution of the story. After all the ups and down, you want the hero to win. You want the bad guys to lose, and the guide...whatever happens to the guide? It doesn't matter because it's not about the guide. It's about the hero. That sense of completion and satisfaction that the story has been resolved is the movement from Buy-in to Ownership. That's presenting.

1. **Positioning**: Attention to Interest
2. **Exploring**: Interest to Buy-in
3. **Presenting**: Buy-in to Ownership

I'll unpack these a bit more here. As you go, you will see how you can quickly adapt these movements to your context.

Movement One - Positioning: Attention to Interest

If you stop and think about it, the first thing you need to do is to get your prospect's attention, right? If they don't see you or hear you, you can't even start the journey. There's a ton of advice for how to do this. Most draw on the things that probably annoy you about sales. Think Arnold Horshack, from *Welcome Back, Kotter*, who was always raising his hand to be picked, shouting, "Ooh, ooh, ooh, ooh!". Google "Horshack ooh ooh," to see a YouTube clip on this. You may get a good laugh.

Getting someone's attention in a way that feels good for you and for your customer is just the beginning. You also need to get their interest. That is, you need to get them interested in *working with you.* How do you get them interested in going on a journey with you? This will be unpacked in the pages ahead. For now, remember positioning is the movement from Attention to Interest. Like a movie trailer, you will see how you can have your prospects saying, "I want to learn more."

Movement Two - Exploring: Interest to Buy-in

Once you have someone's interest in working with you, how do you get their buy-in? What is buy-in? Buy-in is when your prospect moves toward deeper engagement. They want to go on a journey with you because they see you as a potential solution to their problem. Put another way, they've agreed to watch the movie. This typically requires a conversation of some sort to learn more about your prospect's situation.

Prospects want to feel safe with you. Because of this, you need a sales approach that ensures you're acting with honesty and integrity. You will learn how to create a psychologically safe environment that allows your prospect to go deeper with you. You will be exploring in such a way as to help them move from Interest to Buy-in. You'll be able to do it in a way that feels good.

Movement Three - Presenting: Buy-in to Ownership

The third movement empowers you to help others with owning the decision to work with you. This one trips a lot of people up. How do you get your prospects to make the decision to purchase your products and/or service for themselves? That's the big question! It's a question that changes everything. Pressuring people doesn't feel good. You certainly don't want to manipulate anyone. Rather, you want to maintain a positive and healthy relationship with your prospects (and hopefully soon-to-be clients).

To do this, you need to help your prospect own the decision to buy your services. In this movement, you've already got their buy-in, but now what? How do you help your prospect say, "Let's do it!" This is one of the more elusive components in the sales journey. It's also simpler than many make it out to be and something you can learn to do quite easily and with integrity. More good news is that this three-part sales approach helps you to eliminate a lot of the things that don't feel good about sales! More to come on this. Remember: presenting is movement three that helps you help your prospect move from Buy-in to Ownership.

Unlike other sales systems that take a linear and often dogmatic approach, these three movements sit inside the larger and much more flexible sales framework of PEP. Everything in sales can be placed under positioning, exploring, and presenting.

Understanding where your prospect is in their journey will help you better help them. Here's an overview of PEP to help you absorb it.

---

1. Positioning - this is the practice of positioning you well so a prospect notices you and is intrigued by your services. This is the movement of Attention to Interest

2. Exploring - this is the practice of exploring need by creating a safe environment to uncover what matters to your prospect, and if and how you can help your prospect. This is the movement of Interest to Buy-in

3. Presenting - this is the process of presenting a solution in such a way that your prospect owns the decision for themselves. This is the movement from Buy-in to Ownership

---

Your prospect is a human. While I've laid out a linear path for the purposes of understanding the components of PEP, your prospect may be in any of these stages (or all of them) at any given time. PEP allows you the freedom and flexibility to provide some structure in the messiness of your prospect's journey. Put another way, for selling to feel good, you need to "be like water," to quote Bruce Lee. That is, instead of forcing or following a rigid system, you need to be fluid, adapting to your context and flowing with your prospect on their journey. This isn't anything mystical. This is how our brains are literally wired as humans. According to neuroscientist, David Eagleman, the human brain is not "inflexible hardware," instead it "adapts to the world around it." When you are trapped in an inflexible sales system, selling feels forced and uncomfortable. The principles in PEP provide you the ability to adapt and flex to your context.

With this high-level overview in mind, let's look at how you can actually do this in your specific context.

PART TWO

POSITIONING
Positioning You to Stand Out

Chapter 5

Your Public Service Announcement

What is your public service announcement? That is, what is it that you want people to know you can help them with? What problem do you solve for them? What solution are you providing? What do you want them to do? I'm using this well-known concept of a public service announcement as it provides you with a simple and time-tested framework to clarify your message. In fact, I've turned this into an acronym with different words that will help you get clear on what you're selling and why people should care. A public service announcement highlights the Problem, the Solution, and the Action to take. What I call a PSA.

A public service announcement does three things really well:

1. Alerts you to a **problem**
2. Provides you with a **solution**

3. Tells you to take an **action**

If I were to spell out the PSA for COVID 19 it was essentially:

1. **Problem**: Virus is a problem
2. **Solution**: Vaccine is the solution
3. **Action**: Get vaccinated

Commercials and advertisements follow the same pattern.

1. **Problem**: Dirty kitchen floors are ugly
2. **Solution**: Turbo Mop makes cleaning fast & easy
3. **Action**: Buy the mop

This is not a new or revolutionary formula. Sales people have used this pattern for ages. However, as you know, many employ manipulation and pressure which doesn't feel good to people. Think of the old traveling salesman who has the magic elixir for every ailment. Headache problem? Magic elixir is the solution. Give me $X (action) and I'll solve that problem. While solving problems is a good thing, using manipulation and high pressure is not. So, how do you avoid the sales tactics that don't feel good?

1. **Problem**: selling doesn't feel good
2. **Solution**: a different approach to sales
3. **Action**: keep reading

See what I did?

I've identified a problem in sales. The problem is off-putting sales tactics in all their various shapes and sizes. I've felt it. You've felt it. Customers have certainly felt it.

The solution to this problem is that we need to approach sales in a new and different way.

Based on the problem that I have identified and the solution I've created, what do I want people to do? I want them to read my book so they can adopt a new way of selling that feels good. I also want them to take my upcoming sales training course. I want to fix the problem by helping people sell well and to avoid bad sales habits so they can increase their sales and keep their integrity.

This is a good and noble cause. I feel good about selling this solution to the world.

The good news is this: when you are clear on the problem you can help people with, you will feel good. When you are confident in the solution you provide, you will feel good. When you provide an action for your prospect to take - whether they take it *OR NOT* - you will feel good because you did your best to help.

Selling feels bad or "salesy" when you focus on you, your product, or your company. Selling feels good when you talk about the problem you solve for people.

To help, here's an example of the PSA framework for an accounting firm. I picked something boring to show how the PSA makes all the difference.

The pre-work is easy. In this case, I'll think about the concerns people have with taxes. For instance, I don't know many people that enjoy paying or doing their taxes. Taxes are complicated. It can be overwhelming. It's frustrating. There's even a time limit which adds pressure. The risk of an audit looms over you like a dark shadow. These are just a few concerns I came up with off-the-cuff.

So, if I'm a tax consultant, I want to solve the problems my customers experience. It might sound like this.

Problem: Taxes are hard enough and no one wants the headache of an audit.

Solution: We get it. We help our clients breeze through the tax season with our 1-2-3 Tax System so they can enjoy their families.

Action: Call us today.

You can make your PSA shorter or longer. It can be used everywhere - in your prospecting, marketing, website, emails, and sales conversations. It will feel good, too, because you're focused on helping people solve a problem instead of focusing on you.

Here's a simple way to create a PSA. Answer these three questions::

1. Problem: What problem do you solve for your customer?

This is not your title, product, or company. Rather, what do you help your customer to:

- Reduce
- Overcome
- Eliminate
- Stop
- Avoid
- Clarify
- Breakthrough
- Remove
- Simplify

Some of these things will likely be:

- ROI, costs, bottom line
- Brand, reputation, legacy
- Risk, security, safety
- Leverage, growth, ease
- Time, bandwidth, productivity
- Morale, joy, engagement
- Etc...

Here's an example from the tax consultant again:

You know how tax season can be hard and overwhelming, sucking the joy out of your life? We help our customers reduce tax headaches, mitigate risk, and avoid tax audits.

These are problems worth solving!

2. Solution: How do you help them do that?

Your answer to question two regarding your solution is just as important. This is often where salespeople get lost in the details and minutia of their solution. This is bad. It only confuses your prospect. Instead, lay out a clear and simple path to a better future that mitigates risk and ensures their success.

For the tax consultant, it might sound like this: Rather than you getting bogged down in tax paperwork and process:

1. We take care of the details from A to Z
2. This saves you time and reduces your risk of an audit
3. Which enables you to have peace of mind and focus on your business

What will a prospect hear? They'll hear they don't have to worry. Everything will be taken care of. They're in good hands.

By contrast, if the tax consultant started talking about tax forms, receipts, new regulations and tax codes, the prospect would likely have felt overwhelmed, nervous, or anxious.

Keep your solution simple.

Action: What should your prospect do?

Whether you're having a sales conversation, giving a talk, or someone is browsing your website, make it clear what they should do next.

It might be:

"Schedule a Free Tax Consult"

Whatever it is, make it clear.

***

The PSA framework allows you to articulate your value proposition clearly. However, what if you don't feel good about what you're selling? Here are three things to consider:

1. Is it the sales approach? Does it use poor practices and sales tactics? If so, this book will help.

2. Is it belief - i.e., you don't think the product or service actually helps people? If this is indeed the case, creating an action plan to move into something you can believe in would be a great step to take.

3. Can you reframe the problem? Getting at the deeper why of what you do can help you rethink what you do. If you're selling software, are you selling a tool that creates some efficiencies or does your software break down silos in an organization so

people can unleash the full brain power of the company? See the difference? Check out Simon Sinek and The Golden Circle for more on this line of thinking.

Your PSA allows you to get clear on the problem you solve for people. When you're clear on the problem you solve, you'll feel good because you'll have more confidence you can help. You won't be guessing. You can simply say, "I solve this problem with this solution. You can too if you take this action."

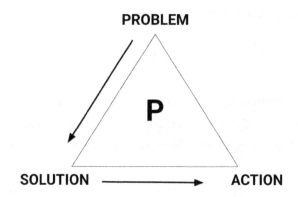

Your PSA, while critical, is not enough. There may be lots of folks who solve the same problem as you do. To help you address this, you need to understand how humans think.

Chapter 6

The Power of Contrast

You are likely familiar with the sales and marketing techniques that vie for your attention. Whether it's a click bait headline on the Internet or a flashing neon sign on the side of the road, businesses are desperate to draw you in. Many of the approaches do not feel good. Don't worry. You won't have to resort to tacky tactics. In sales, you'll find free trials, free samples, and lots of big promises to get your attention. These are not necessarily bad. Rather, the trouble with all of this is that it's just noise among noise. Your prospects are so bombarded with these techniques that they become immune to the noise. This makes it hard for them to see you. Yet, one simple fact is the key: *To stand out to your prospects, you have to be different.*

What's the simplest way to be different? What's so simple and right in front of us all the time?

Contrast.

You have to contrast with something. Let me show you what I mean right now. TO STAND OUT YOU HAVE TO CONTRAST. Do you see what I did there? This is an example of contrasting UPPER CASE to lower case. Is it that simple? Actually, yes. Why does this work? It works because that's how the human brain is wired. If you can learn to speak to the appropriate parts of the brain, then you will capture your prospect's attention more effectively. You can learn to speak human.

What does it mean to speak human? In order to help people, they need to hear you. Most salespeople I come across in my training love to talk. What they fail to recognize is that their prospects are not listening. For prospects to hear you, you need to speak in a way that resonates with them. Specifically, it means speaking to a certain part of the brain. For a good book on this, check out *The Persuasion Code,* by authors Christophe Morin and Patrick Renovoise. I'll provide some highlights of their work. In short, you can split the brain into two parts - the primal brain and the rational brain. To grab your prospect's attention, you need to speak to the primal brain. This helps them see you better. How does this relate to contrast? I'm getting there. According to Morin and Renovoise, the primal brain responds to six core stimuli. The six stimuli are things that are **contrastable, tangible, personal, memorable,**

visual, and **emotional**. In my experience with sales, **contrast** is the mother of them all. It's also one of the easiest to employ. In this part of the journey with your prospect (the movement from Attention to Interest), it helps to speak to the primal brain using contrast.

Most salespeople speak to the rational brain. They'll quote numbers, statistics, and features. These are things that the rational brain is quite good at understanding. To be clear, there is a time and place for stats, but it is typically much later in the sales journey.

Hints of these two different parts of the brain are described in the common sales refrain, "People buy on emotion and justify it with logic." Put in context, it's the primal brain we need to speak to first, then the rational brain. When salespeople start at the rational brain, quoting stats, features, benefits, and numbers, the prospect's rational brain is busy doing mental gymnastics to see if what you're saying even makes sense. Instead, your prospect needs to see you first as someone who can help them get where they want to go. This requires speaking to the primal brain.

Interestingly, salespeople will often get super-excited during their pitch to a prospect. They're often thinking that they're giving a stellar sales presentation. They know their product well so they highlight stats and figures and all the cool bells and whistles. What they do not realize is that the stats and figures are only rationalizing their own choice to continue to sell the product and/or service. They forget that the prospect isn't there yet. The prospect hasn't made that move. Instead of actually moving their prospect from Attention to Interest, these annoying sales habits inhibit a salesperson's ability to be heard, let alone be seen as a trusted guide.

Let me pause here for a minute. Is the idea of speaking to the primal brain resonating with you, or does it seem manipulative? I promise you that manipulation is not the intent. The intent in stimulating certain parts of the brain is so your prospect can actually hear you. You need to give them an opportunity to take the journey with you.

Maya Angalou said it best:

> "I've learned that people will forget what you said, people will forget what you did, but people will never forget how you made them feel."

Maya's famous quote is speaking about the primal part of the brain. As I've played out past sales conversations in my head, I've realized that I was really good at speaking to the rational brain. However, and I hated to admit it, I was weak on the primal side - the emotional side. I cannot overstate the importance of understanding this.

To help you avoid this all-too-common pitfall, let's look at a great example of speaking human through the power of contrast.

Remember those "I'm a Mac" and "I'm a PC" ads from Apple Computers? There was one in particular in which the PC guy is dressed in a white hospital gown. He's slumped forward, overweight, and generally quite sickly. He's also wearing glasses, a watch, black socks and wingtips. To top it off, he's got a toupee. By contrast, the Apple guy is wearing all black, standing in a confident and relaxed power pose. He's at ease with the world. Why did Apple's marketing team use contrast in this way? Apple could have quoted stat after stat and feature after feature. But they didn't do that. Instead, Apple tapped into the primal brain of its buyers using contrast. This contrast triggered the other five stimuli outlined by Morin and Renovoise.

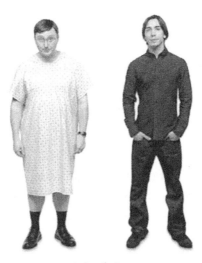

© Apple Inc.

Here's a breakdown of the ad so you can see the power of contrast:

Contrast: The Mac guy was depicted as young and cool. The actor was dressed in slick black. He was confident. He stood tall. He was calm. His hands rested casually in his pockets. He was healthy. In contrast, the PC guy was the complete opposite of all these things, looking defeated, weak, sickly, and nerdy!

Tangible: The Apple ad is so tangible and clear that it is understood instantly (and subconsciously). You didn't need to be taught anything. It just made sense. You didn't even need to articulate the message. The contrast was so striking that your brain recognized, received, and remembered the point being made.

Personal: The contrast made the ad personal. Everyone wants to be cool, relaxed, confident, and casual. Remember high school? And you've likely worn a poorly fitting hospital gown at one time or another. How did that make you feel? Vulnerable? Exposed? Anxious? Drafty? All the above? Again, the contrast was real. You don't want to be the sickly PC Guy. You want to be the cool, hip, and healthy Mac guy.

Memorable: The fact that people still watch Mac ads years later proves the staying power of speaking to the primal brain. No one is rewatching PC ads. The power of contrast sticks in your memory.

Visual: Of course the ad was visual. The contrasting personas, postures, accessories, and clothing told more of the story than the words did. You were understanding the message more with your eyes than the actual words being spoken. Why are visuals so powerful? Vision is located in the primal brain.

Emotional: All of this was making the ads very emotional. Not only were they funny, Apple knew that deep down you want to be ranked among the cool kids. You want to be seen as put together, confident, and at ease in the world. You don't want to be the vulnerable, sick, nervous nerd.

That's the power of contrast.

Put in your sales context, it is the power of speaking human so your prospect hears you. That is the power of CONTRAST. While you can certainly work to incorporate all six stimuli into your sales and marketing efforts, contrast is the one to master. You will see this in the examples ahead.

One more thought about contrast. Think about how primal it really is. Contrast is happening right now with the words on these pages. The black type on the white page is only visible to you because of contrast. If I typed the letters in white, you wouldn't be able to see the words. In the same way, if you sound like every other salesperson speaking to the rational brain, or if you're talking about yourself rather than making your prospect the hero, your prospect will not hear you.

Below are three simple examples to incorporate contrast into your conversations starting today:

1. In contrast to other sales books filled with manipulative tactics, this sales approach allows you to keep your integrity, avoid off-putting sales techniques, and to win more business.

2. Unlike traditional consulting techniques that take twelve or even eighteen months to see a return, our approach provides you quick wins within the first sixty days and lays out a path to continuously deliver value over the course of the engagement.

3. Rather than outdated CRM systems that cause employee frustration, disengagement, which leads to inaccurate data, our CRM was built by employees and gamified to maximize data integrity and employee engagement.

Did you notice the three opening phrases? I used contrast words. Phrases such as *in contrast to*, *unlike*, and *rather than* hit the primal brain and clarify what you're saying. They create context for your prospect. Put more artistically, they create a canvas upon which you can paint a vision that invites your prospect to enter. Doing this allows them to hear you. They will be able to engage with what you're saying much more easily.

Watch what happens when I remove contrast:

"I help sales people avoid off-putting and annoying sales techniques."

It's okay, but it doesn't pack much of a punch, does it? It's harder to hear. There is not enough contrast.

You don't want to make it hard for your prospects to know what you do. Contrast helps you to be heard and understood. It's easy to use. It also feels good when your prospect understands and says, "Oh, I get it - cool!"

Chapter 7

The Power of Reframe

Reframe is the idea of helping people see things in a different light. It's not a new concept. There's even a popular improv game based on this. One person starts every sentence with either "Fortunately," or "Unfortunately." For example, player one might say, "Unfortunately, it looks like it's going to rain!" Player two might say, "Fortunately, we get to test out our new umbrellas!" Another example could be related to this book. "Unfortunately, you have to put up with me and the ideas in this book." You might say (hopefully), "Fortunately, it will help me help people more effectively!" Reframe is a simple, but powerful idea to help your prospects. Done well, it's one of the greatest feelings you can experience in sales because you've helped enlighten someone.

The idea of reframe, in modern-day sales anyway, was popularized by the Challenger sales books. There are two of them: *The Challenger Sale* and *The Challenger Customer*. Like the other book titles I listed earlier, these titles may trigger an allergic reaction in you. You might be thinking, "Do I have to challenge people; can't I just be nice?" Nevertheless, these two are worth a read. But if you want to know who the real masters of the reframe are, it's politicians. Please note: we will **not** be learning to use reframes in the sometimes manipulative ways that politicians do. However, politicians do provide us with some good examples as we learn about the power of reframe.

There's a classic example from politics that illustrates the power of a reframe. During the 1984 presidential campaign, there was concern about Ronald Reagan's age. In a debate with Walter Mondale, Reagan was asked a question that implied he might be too old to handle the pressures of the office. Reagan reframed the situation by stating:

> "I will not make age an issue of this campaign. I am not going to exploit, for political purposes, my opponent's youth and inexperience."

See what he did? That's a reframe. You can Google "Reagan, Mondale Age Issue" and watch the short clip - it's worth it to see the audience's (and Mondale's) reaction. The point: Reagan could have gone down the rabbit hole of age. He could have defended himself. He could have justified his leadership abilities. All he would have done, though, is draw even more attention to the concern. Instead, he turned *age* into *experience*. He reframed the story. The issue was settled.

While politicians provide us wonderful reframe examples, too often they are meant for political ends rather than actually helping people. In sales, the reframe should be used to help people see things in a new way. Why? Simple. Our prospects are stuck. They can't see a way out. They have tunnel vision. They may not even know there is a different way to think about something or a solution to address their problem. They need help. They need a breath of fresh air. If you use reframe in this way, you can help your prospect to get unstuck and to see their situation in a new light. As a result, you will be seen as a trusted guide, helping someone to imagine new possibilities, rather than a manipulative salesperson pushing an agenda. This feels good.

I'll list six reframe examples below. The words and phrases are likely familiar to you. Don't underestimate them because of their simplicity or familiarity. They're very effective in helping prospects get unstuck and to see things anew.

1. "The good news is…" This simple statement shifts the focus to possibilities. It's a contrasting statement that helps focus the brain on solutions instead of getting stuck in worry and anxiety. It might sound like this when you are talking with a prospect: "I appreciate the situation you are currently experiencing and the scenarios you described to me. The good news is that you have a firm grasp of these realities and are taking steps to move forward." Can you see how this might shine a light into the darkness that your prospect is experiencing?

2. "Imagine..." Like "good news," this word encourages people to think about possibilities instead of problems. One of my mentors would always say to me when I was struggling with sales targets or with my team, "Ted, imagine if this works!" What he was doing was focusing me on the things I could do and grounding my thinking in hope. Nelson Mandela said, "May your choices reflect your hopes, not your fears." That's what my mentor was doing - reframing my fear to hope. With your prospect, it might sound like this: "Imagine having the ability to X, Y, and Z. Would that be helpful in your context, or am I off base?" Do you see what this does? It casts vision and hope to help move your prospect toward something better.

3. "When I talk with others in your position..." This phrase has two powerful advantages. The first is that no one wants to be alone. That is, to know that others are in a similar situation is comforting and allows prospects to begin to think about possibilities. It puts the prospect at ease so they can hear what you have to say that may help them think differently.

The second is that when folks are in a tough spot, they want to talk with someone who has been there - a trusted guide. When you say this, you're telling your prospect I've seen this. I've been there. I can guide you to the other side. It might sound like this: "When I talk with other CEOs, they tell me they're experiencing X, Y, and Z. Is any of this on your mind, or not so much?" This simple question helps your prospect begin talking about the things they need to tackle (the dragons they need to slay). This opens the door to possibility. You'll learn to guide them on this journey in the chapters ahead.

4. "Rather than…" These two words trigger the primal brain with contrast. Remember, the primal brain is really good at recognizing and absorbing things that contrast. Contrast can help your prospect hear your reframe. It might sound like this in a sales conversation: "Rather than traditional solutions which can take a lot of time and resources, our clients appreciate the fact that they can do X, Y, and Z." What this statement is doing is using contrast to help a prospect see that old outdated ways are not the path. It's time for something new. It's time to look at things differently. It's important to remember this is not manipulation. Here's why. Status quo - doing things the same old way - is a powerful force that can keep your prospects pinned down and stuck. Helping your prospect break through that is part of your responsibility as a trusted guide. When your customer says, "I never thought of it that way," it feels good. Whether they buy from you or not, you've just expanded someone's horizons.

5. "Our approach is a little different…" This is one of my favorite things to say for two reasons. The first is that things that are different stand out. They get noticed. If I "wRItE liKe ThIs" (just by changing where I capitalized the letters), you'll notice. It's unique. It's different. So, when you say, "Our approach is a little different" in your sales conversations (provided that it is true, of course), your prospect's primal brain will notice and be ready to listen; you'll stand out. It might sound like this: "Our approach is a little different, and it's not for everyone. If it resonates with you, wonderful; if not, that's okay too and we can part as friends."

Statements like this are controversial in many sales circles. I've had people interrupt my sales training to say, "Why the heck would I ever want to potentially minimize my services or give my prospect an out?" It's a fair question. Why would you? What they fail to recognize is that they're assuming their services are what the prospect wants. Assumptions are always dangerous. In other words, this objection comes from the misguided idea that they control the prospect, and thus they need to manipulate and cajole. They do not recognize that it's the prospect's job to make the decision. They do not realize that they're the guide. They're trying to win rather than help their prospect to win.

The second thing I like about this is that it encourages you to truly offer something different and unique. It may be amazing customer service. It may be speed. It may be a simpler product or approach. Perhaps it's taking a problem and turning it on its head. Perhaps it's you. Whatever it is, it's an opportunity to help people see you and their situation in a new way.

6. "This may not resonate with you…" What I'm about to say may not resonate with you. In fact, some salespeople resist this particular phrase. If it irks you, don't use it. However, I would encourage you to stay open-minded. This simple phrase is powerful. It does two major things. One: it puts the prospect at ease because it removes pressure, which opens the door for a reframe. It provides the prospect the freedom to engage or not. This will feel good for them. Two: it puts you in the position of not assuming. It will help you to remain curious and open to hearing what matters to your prospect (which is always good practice for salespeople).

I'll put all six together so you can hear it for yourself. Then you can decide if you want to incorporate this language into your sales conversations - or not. Totally up to you. It's important to note that they are not meant to be used all at once. I'm just doing it below to show you how natural it all sounds to help reframe your prospects to see things in a new way.

Ready?

The good news is that this sales book takes a unique approach. It helps folks to sell honestly, avoiding the sales tactics that are so off-putting. **Rather than** traditional sales techniques and tactics that tend to manipulate people, the principles in this book allow for more natural and free-flowing conversations with prospects. The methodology outlined ahead is *a little different*. *It may not resonate with you* and that's okay. The reality is that *when I talk with other people like yourself*, some, not all, tell me that they're either leery of sales systems, or weary of techniques that go against their values as a human being. *Imagine* if sales didn't have to be the high pressure tactics of old! Instead, you could be seen as a trusted guide in the eyes of your prospects. Would that be helpful in your context, or am I off base?"

I hope this gives you a taste of how these words and phrases might help you reframe so you can better help your prospects.

There's another tool that can help you help your prospects see things differently. Questions. We'll cover how to ask good questions ahead. But for now, questions have the ability to open new possibilities and ideas. Hal Gregersen writes:

> "Questions...prove catalytic. They dissolve barriers to thinking, like limiting prior assumptions, and they channel creative energy down more productive pathways. People who have been feeling stuck suddenly see new possibilities and are motivated to pursue them."

I'll share one powerful example of this. A sales mentor of mine was helping an organization quantify the cost of disengagement. He asked, "Can you help me understand what this situation is costing the organization?" The prospect responded, "No, I haven't done the math on that." He replied, "No problem, what would you guess?" The prospect stated that they were not comfortable guessing. He said, "Totally get it. Could you throw a dart?" The prospect said, "No, I'd be afraid of being too far off." My mentor paused and asked, "What would it be if you did know?" Without missing a beat, the prospect said, "Oh, easily 3-4 million per year!"

The lesson?

The right questions can reframe and help people break through.

Remember, at this stage, you are seeking to help your prospect move from Attention to Interest. You want your prospects to see you, your services, and their situation in a different light. To be clear, both contrast and reframe can be used in any stage of the PEP framework - not just Positioning. In the next chapter you will learn how to go a level deeper with your PSA to really engage your prospects.

Reframing phrases:

1. The good news is...
2. Imagine...
3. When I talk with others in your position...
4. Rather than...
5. Our approach is a little different...
6. This may not resonate with you...

Chapter 8

Helping You Stand Out

When you think about positioning yourself and your services it is tempting to want to tell your story. It's natural. You're excited. You care about what you do. You want others to get it. You may even think that's what you're supposed to do. I mean, how else would your prospect know what you do if you don't talk about what you do, right? Wrong. Your prospect's primary concern (rightfully so), is how you can help them. When you talk about you, you put yourself in the hero position. This is where everyone goes wrong. Let me show you. It sounds like this:

"Hi, my name is Ted. I work at Boring, Blah, & Ugh. I focus on marketing, messaging, sales enablement, and sales training."

Yawn!

That is indeed what I do.

However, it's not going to capture anyone's attention.

Do you think a prospect could find themselves in that positioning statement? No. It does not address the primal brain and capture the prospect's attention.

Now, you may be asking, "How do I stand out if it's all about them?"

Great question!

Remember that you are the guide. There is a hard reality that many wrestle with: prospects don't care about you. They care about what you can do for *them*. It's the "What's in it for me?" (WIIFM) reality. As you read that opening sentence of my pitch, did you see yourself in the story? No. You couldn't. I made it all about me. You don't care about me. You care about you. That's okay. In the same way, prospects do not care about you. They care about themselves. This is normal. When you're in the prospect seat you think the same way. So, instead of using a positioning framework that is focused on you and what you do, flip the story to your prospect and focus on the problem you solve for them and what they would have the ability to do with your help.

Doing this will help you feel good about selling. Let's look again at the principles and framework to create an attention-getting PSA.

Here's an example:

1. Problem: Start by describing what happens when someone works with you (not what you do). That is, you don't tell someone your job title or the ins and outs of your work. That's actually boring (unless you're an astronaut - then it's totally cool). Instead, tell them the problem you solve for them. It might sound like this:

"You know those manipulative sales tactics that no one likes? They're uncomfortable. They don't feel good to anyone. I provide an approach that allows sellers to avoid that stuff so they can close more deals and keep their integrity."

Did you see yourself in that positioning statement? Of course! I made what I do about you.

2. Solution: You'll want a short and clear solution to the problem you solve. When you hit on a problem that matters to your prospect, lay out an easy-to-follow path to your solution. It helps to use contrast and reframe and to cast a vision of what life will be like with your solution. It might sound like this:

"My approach is a little different. Rather than outdated sales methodologies, I provide a three-step framework that will help you feel good about selling. Imagine having the confidence and the words to engage your prospects respectfully. In this way, they see you as a trusted resource allowing you to win more business."

Notice that I built off the problem. The problem is people don't feel good about selling. The solution is my three-step framework. I also reframed, casting a vision of what life could be like. Why? People need to see where they're going and what could be. This helps de-risk the decision to work with you. People want to know they're in good hands and will be successful. Give some thought again to how you would answer these questions about your PSA:

- What's the problem you solve for your customers?
- What's the solution?
- What action should they take?

3. Action: What do you want to invite your prospect to do? This is a CTA: a *call to action*. To feel good about selling, you want to invite your prospect to own the action step. It's really a CTO - a *call to ownership*. You want to allow your prospect the freedom to take the journey with you (or not). It might sound like something as simple as this:

"Are you open to a conversation to learn more about you and your situation, or should we end things here?"

If this feels odd to you, that's okay. The good news is that with an open mind and a little practice, it becomes natural.

Let's contrast the typical positioning statements we often hear compared to the PSA framework.

Typical Positioning Statement Format: "Hi, my name is Ted. I work at Boring, Blah, & Ugh. I focus on marketing, messaging, sales enablement, and sales training."

It's very hard for a prospect to see themselves in this.

The response might simple be, "Oh, interesting…"

Now, let's look at the PSA framework.

PSA framework: "You know the awful feelings of manipulative sales tactics that no one likes? Rather than irritating prospects, and doing things that don't feel right, I help sellers close more deals and keep their integrity."

How do you do that, Ted?

"Thanks for asking. The approach is a little different. Instead of outdated sales tactics, I empower sellers with a three-step framework based on core principles. Imagine having the words and the confidence to engage your prospects respectfully so that they see you as a trusted guide, allowing you to win more business."

That's really interesting, Ted. Is this a book, a course, or training series you offer?

"I appreciate you asking. There are a number of options that might align with your goals. Are you open to a conversation to learn more about you and your situation, or not so much?"

No, this sounds great, Ted. Let's set something up.

Did you see and feel the difference? Did it feel sleazy? Was it off-putting? Not at all. It was honest and clear. It puts the focus where it belongs - directly on the needs of the prospect. Will it always go as smoothly as above? No. And it doesn't need to. The PSA combined with the principles of contrast and reframe will help you to stand out. Your prospects will see you as a trusted guide.

These conversations are meant to be natural and fluid with lots of back and forth. Just remember this is the movie trailer. This is the movement of Attention to Interest. Often we want to plow ahead all the way to presenting what we do, but there are some critical steps that need to happen first, and you do not want to skimp on them.

You may have noticed, too, that I asked if they were open to learning more, and open to a conversation. This is intentional. Many sales people come in fast and furious asking for thirty minutes to show you this, that, and the other thing. Asking for time, or asking to schedule some time is actually less effective and can even be off-putting. According to Gong, asking if someone is open to learning more or open to a conversation is twice as likely to get a more favorable response compared to asking for time. Why? Simple. It's less threatening.

Before proceeding to the next section of PEP, Exploring, there are a few pointers on positioning that are worth noting.

Pointer #1 - When you're positioning yourself with a prospect, it is so tempting to start selling. As soon as a prospect expresses interest, you may get excited and start circling around like an excited puppy. This is bad. This is not the calm, trusted guide prospects are looking for. Moreover, your prospect who expressed what you assume to be interest may not be interested at all. The point here is that the positioning part of the journey is not the time to sell. It is not the time for deep discovery questions or for features and benefits. The goal is simple. It is to get enough interest to help your prospect to take a step with you. That is, the goal is to move someone from Attention to Interest. If you go into sales presentation mode, you may kill a deal before it gets off the ground.

Pointer #2 - Your pace matters. Too many salespeople rush through their PSA, making it hard to follow, or worse, they come across like a fast-talking salesperson. There are some simple fixes for this. Practice what I call the "power pause." The power pause is built into the sales principles in this book, but it's worth fleshing out a bit more. In the three steps of your PSA, there are three distinct parts - Problem, Solution, and Action. Each step requires a pause. This allows your prospect (the hero) to participate in the conversation. After you lay out the problem you solve, you should pause and wait. How long? Science points out that after a four second pause, someone will speak. For a great book on this type of data and human interactions check out Jack Schafer's book *The Like Switch*. Four seconds! Isn't that an awkward silence? Yes and no. Yes, because you feel like it is. That's why salespeople keep chattering on and on. And no, because, while it often feels like a long time to you, your prospect may be thinking and processing. This is a vital time for them. The silence allows them both processing time and the opportunity to speak. This is very important. Put another way, creating this space is far more important than avoiding awkwardness.

As you know, salespeople love to talk. They'll often run through every stage of their PSA without taking a breath. There's an underlying belief in sales that if the prospect is letting you talk, they must be interested (at least to some degree). The reality is much simpler. You have not created the space or the environment for a conversation. Instead, you've created a stage for your presentation. This won't feel good. You will feel the pressure to perform. If you don't want to be like the salespeople that annoy you, don't do this. Instead, get comfortable with the power pause. In my experience most salespeople only pause for an average of 0.5 seconds. That's half of one second! In other words, the prospect essentially can't get a word in. You don't need to pause for four seconds - although this can be beneficial at times. A great average according to Gong is one second. I prefer two seconds.

Pointer # 3 - Another area of caution in your sales conversations is "the monologue." Again, salespeople love to talk. If you don't want to sound like the irritating salespeople you've experienced, you need to avoid the monologue. The monologue is just what it sounds like. It's what late night TV show hosts do. While it's perfectly fine for TV, it's horrible for sales. I've heard recordings of sales people talking for over four minutes straight, rambling on and on, jumping from feature to feature, anecdote to anecdote. Meanwhile, they have no idea if what they're saying matters to their prospect at all. The power pause addresses this problem as well.

To avoid the monologue, you can simply add a, "Let me pause here. Is this resonating with you, or am I out in left field?" Your prospect may even chuckle when you say this. Chuckles are good. How long should you talk for? Stay under two minutes (108 seconds according to Gong). What I've found is that this allows for the vital back and forth with you and your prospect. So what should you be doing when you're not talking? Aside from active listening, you want to be asking great questions. You will see how to do this in the next chapter.

Within Positioning, there are a number of principles to help you:

1. Your PSA helps you be clear on how you help people and what they should do about it.
2. Speaking "human" with contrast and reframe helps your prospect to see you and hear you so you have a chance to help them.
3. Avoiding annoying sales habits and instead using good pace, pauses, and demeanor allows your prospect to engage so they can take a step with you.

MOVEMENT ONE	MOVEMENT TWO	MOVEMENT THREE
POSITIONING	**EXPLORING**	**PRESENTING**
Attention → Interest	Interest → Buy-In	Buy-in → Ownership
Positioning you to gain a prospect's interest	Exploring if and how you can help your prospect	Presenting a solution for prospect ownership

```
        PROBLEM
          /\
         /  \
        / P  \
       /_____\
SOLUTION ———▶ ACTION
```

Summary of key principles with Positioning:

PROBLEM: Be crystal clear on the problem you solve for your customers

SOLUTION: Differentiate yourself, providing a clear solution so your prospect can envision a new future state

ACTION: Extend a free-choice invitation to your prospect to take a journey with you

PART THREE

EXPLORING
Exploring Need In A Safe Environment

Chapter 9

How To Have Great Sales Conversations

Great sales conversations don't just happen. Professional salespeople know this and plan accordingly. If you want to feel good about selling, knowing how to have a good sales conversation will help a lot - even if the conversation goes off the rails.

Once you've got your prospect's attention and interest, the next movement to help your prospect on their journey is Exploring. This is the movement from Interest to Buy-in. How do you allow your prospect to freely buy into what you're offering?

I'll outline two approaches. The first is the classic discovery approach. It has lots of names. You may be familiar with such terms as discovery questions, need-based questions, or exploring needs questions. The Sandler Selling System,

MEDDIC, and Miller-Heimann are some great sales approaches when it comes to discovery. In spite of an abundance of resources, though, many salespeople struggle in this area.

The second approach is what I call Rapid Discovery. It's sort of like speed dating discovery. While not new in selling methodologies, it was popularized by Challenger selling which asserts that customers don't actually know what they need and must be challenged to think differently. This leads to a teach, tailor, and take control approach to sales. SPIN selling is another approach that asks a series of questions to help customers come to their own conclusion. Like the classic discovery approach (and like speed dating), many are uncomfortable with this approach, too.

The reality is this: both approaches have the potential to help or hinder the customer, and both may either work well for the seller or create anxiety. If either approach is missing the principles you've learned so far then selling doesn't feel good. These sales approaches are tactical tools to help you help your prospect move along the journey. Either one can be used in the three-part sales framework I've laid out. In fact, both are needed. Author Tony Gambill calls this the balance between "telling and asking." The secret is knowing when to use which approach. Your context will dictate which approach will need to be emphasized.

To be clear, sometimes no discovery is needed. I know discovery is a sacred cow in sales, but context matters, relationships matter, and the world is changing. A lot of sales are transactional, requiring zero discovery. Sometimes the existing relationships between buyer and seller suffice. I was chatting with a buyer who knew me from a past life. I was only able to get out two discovery questions because she talked for twenty-seven minutes straight. At the end, I said, this is my approach - do you think that will help in your context or not so much. She said, "Absolutely, how should I pay you?" Moreover, free trials now allow prospects to discover all on their own. And many consulting engagements have paid discovery phases. Discovery has quite a range. There is no right way. That said, there are principles at play, and it's still important to have an approach. I'll teach you how I use both the classic discovery approach and the rapid discovery approach.

Here's a simple way to help you know which approach may work better in your context - at least at a high level.

Classic Discovery Approach - use when your prospect's problems are complex, as with larger or enterprise organizations.

In these situations, you'll need to do some digging to unearth the dynamics at play. This is critical. Asking the right questions can even have a therapeutic effect on your prospects. They may not have even realized the depths of what's at stake or had time to think it through. Helping someone in this way feels really good. You're like a therapist.

Getting to the root of an organization's challenges is important, but they still need to do something about it. What can catch salespeople by surprise is that their customers may not be willing to change, despite the seriousness of their situation. In the *The Leadership Triangle*, the authors point out that there are three sides at play at any given time: a tactical side, a strategic side, and a transformational side. It's this last one where discovery approaches may fall short. You can present the best case in the world both strategically and tactically based on your discovery, but if you're not helping folks transform their thinking, it won't end well.

Rapid Discovery Approach - use when your solution is new, unique, and/or different, or the problems are known, allowing you to educate on a new approach or advantage.

The Rapid Discovery approach is about educating your prospect. It is very effective when the problem is clear and the ramifications are known. For example, turnover in retail is a known problem. There may not be a need to go deep with discovery questions. In fact, prospects may get annoyed and feel like you're manipulating them with a barrage of questions. Instead, educating them about a new or unique approach that solves their problem may help them to think differently. Prospects will even welcome the insights. Business leaders are always open to new ideas that will help them be more effective. It feels good to help people think about things in a fresh way. You will, of course, need to ask questions, but the emphasis is educational.

Interestingly, everyone agrees that getting under the surface of prospect concerns to unearth root causes is vital. It's built into every sales methodology. Yet, despite the importance of the exploration step in the sales process, it is one that is most often skipped or covered insufficiently.

Why?

It's the hardest part in the sales journey. The hardest part of any journey is the middle. You can't turn back, and you can't quite see the finish line.

Exploring demands patience, empathy, and a clear path. Because of this, many salespeople rush through this step or skip over it completely. Unfortunately, this can create serious problems for you.

Imagine walking into your doctor's office and saying, "My arm hurts." Suddenly, the doctor gets a gleam in her eye and exclaims, "Let me show you my operating room, scalpel, and anesthesia!" I suspect that would make you pretty uncomfortable. In fact, it's downright creepy. Yet, this is common in sales. Salespeople get a little bit of interest from a prospect and they jump all the way to solutions without first understanding the problem fully.

This is sales malpractice.

Instead, you need to slow down and ask questions. A good doctor will ask many probing questions about your arm before recommending a course of treatment. As a salesperson, you, too, will need to ask questions to get under the surface. To be a trusted guide, you need to learn to ask good questions. You also need to listen to the answers in order to understand root issues. This isn't as hard as most sales systems make it out to be. So, how do you get under the surface?

Three levels of pain

Most salespeople rarely get past surface level pain. That is, they rarely get past, "my arm hurts," before launching into some sales pitch. They simply take the surface pain and run. You can do better than this by understanding the three levels of pain.

The three levels of pain were popularized by GuruGanesha Khalsa, founder of the *Conscious Selling System*. They are: Technical, Business, and Personal.

Here's an easy way to think about these levels:

1. **Surface**: This is surface level pain - what doctors call "presenting pain" (e.g., my arm hurts). It's a technical concern. You want your arm to work correctly, right? It's the same when exploring business problems. Your prospect may want a new CRM or higher employee engagement - that's the technical need. You, as a trusted guide, will need to discover the why behind this technical need in order to best serve them. This leads to business impact.

2. **Business Impact**: This level speaks to the need to quantify the costs to the business. What's the impact of an arm that hurts? Think of it this way. If a carpenter has a problem with their arm, they may be at risk of losing $100,000 annually. In business, if you need a new CRM because the old one is not allowing you to track your customers the way you need in order to drive revenue, it could cost you $1,000,000 annually. It may also be taxing your IT and customer service teams and hurting your Glassdoor ratings, which is making it hard to recruit new talent and so on. That's the business impact.

3. **Personal**: This explores why addressing the situation matters to your prospect on a personal level. The carpenter may lose their job and their family may suffer. Those are serious concerns. In the case of the business with the outdated CRM, the reputation and future of the business may be at risk. This is likely top of mind for your prospect whose job may be on the line, or who wants to feel like the hero and save the day.

How do you walk a prospect through these levels of pain in a way that is respectful and honors their journey? Opinions vary so widely it's hard to keep track. The good news is you can bypass a lot of sales mistakes by understanding a little psychology.

Too often salespeople ask leading or presumptive questions when exploring a prospect's context. These are likely the questions that do not sit well with you. For example:

- *What are the top problems keeping you up at night?*

- *Is saving 25% meaningful to you?*
- *What business challenges are you experiencing?*

These questions *can* work in some contexts, but they can also trigger a negative response from your prospect. Your prospect could easily respond with, "I don't know if I'd call them problems." Or, "Of course - who wouldn't want to save 25%! Do you think I'm an idiot?" Or they might respond with, "I'm not sure I'd call them challenges." In short, these questions risk breaking trust. They tend to corner your prospect and can cause them to lash out. There's a term psychologists use for this from J.W. Brehm's work in the 1960s. It's called **psychological reactance**, which is defined as:

> *An unpleasant motivational arousal that emerges when people experience a threat to or loss of their free behaviors. It serves as a motivator to restore one's freedom.*

Put another way, it's the feeling of being cornered like a wild animal and having the desire to strike out. Let me put this in the context of sales. I will trigger reactance in you right now by using some common sales approaches that you may have experienced yourself.

Ready?

"I think this sales approach will be exactly what you need to solve all your issues and problems. You could get your whole team up to speed, selling like mad, and avoid all those challenges you're having with your company. Don't you want to increase your sales performance?"

How do you feel? Empowered and free or annoyed and diminished?

Let's just pause here and notice some of the words from Brhem's definition that can be used to describe the prospect's state of mind when psychological reactance is triggered. After these types of sales conversations, notice that reactance produces **unpleasant** feelings. You're seen as a **threat**, undermining the very foundations of trust. Rather than helping your prospect see the value of you and your product or service, you are forcing them to restore their human need to exert **free behaviors**.

Poor sales conversations are just that: poor. They undermine trust because they limit a fundamental drive to be human: freedom. This doesn't feel good for anyone. The good news is that sales conversations do not have to be this way.

Two Frameworks for Great Sales Conversations

Whether using the classic discovery approach, rapid discovery approach, or a combination of both, you need to guide your prospects in a way that helps them unpack what's important to them. There are two distinct parts to discovery conversations:

1. The first is understanding what's important to your prospect.

2. The second is a conversation about a potential solution.

There are a total of six steps. Part one has three steps. Part two has three steps. Here's part one:

Classic Discovery Framework

1. A simple opener
2. Six follow-up questions
3. Recap & transition

A Simple Opener

To begin a great sales conversation, start with what matters to your prospect. Like your PSA, you want to start with the problem your customer is experiencing. Keep the focus on them. It might sound like this:

"I'm not sure this is your experience, but when I talk with other leaders in your position they tell me that they are:

1. Experiencing this…
2. Seeing that…
3. And still feeling the effects of…

Is any of this on your mind, or am I off base?"

What's happening in this simple opener? There are two key things.

1. I'm creating safety. I'm letting the prospect know I'm a professional. I've been there. I'm not assuming anything and I can be trusted, e.g., "I talk with other leaders…" I'm essentially saying I may be able to help them given my experience, but I'm exercising humility as I may not understand their context.

2. It's not about me. The conversation is intentionally geared toward what matters to the prospect. It is focused on the problems my prospect may be experiencing.

This approach may feel awkward at first. That's normal. Discomfort is part of learning something new. **To feel good about selling you have to do things differently.**

You may be concerned that your simple opener won't land with your prospect. Your prospect may say, "Nah, not so much." That's okay. The worst case scenario is this leads to learning what *is* important to your prospect. In other words, even if you got it wrong, your prospect will gladly correct you. They might say, "Actually, I'm struggling with this and that." Isn't that what you really want to do: help someone, if you can, with something that's negatively impacting them? To do that, you have to find out what's important to them in a non-threatening way.

The simple opener gets the conversation started. The following questions will help your prospect find their way through what matters to them. You will help them navigate the three levels of pain discussed earlier.

Six Follow-Up Questions

The six follow up questions are asked in order. They help to create a safe place in which to get under the surface.

The six follow-up questions are:

1. Tell me more...
2. Any specifics or a recent example you can share?
3. How long has this been happening?
4. What have you tried, and how did it work?
5. What's the business impact?
6. Where does this land on your priority list?

I'll walk through each one to provide an idea of how this might sound with your prospect.

1. Tell me more: It might sound like this. "You mentioned x and y are not what they used to be; can you tell me more?" Your prospect will tell you more because this open-ended question invites your prospect to talk about what matters to them. "Tell me more," has been used in psychology for decades to help people find their way. It gives your prospect a safe space in which to open up. Plus, it keeps you from steering the conversation toward what could be your biased agenda.

Now, to be clear, it can get messy. I've had prospects tell me their life story, and I've learned things that had nothing to do with the need they were trying to address. That's okay; sometimes people just need to vent. As their trusted guide, though, you can easily help them to get back on track, and to dig deeper into the things that will help their particular situation.

2. Are there any specifics or recent examples you can share?: Depending on where your prospects ends, you can start with, "I appreciate the specifics; are there any others or perhaps a recent example of what you just described?" Or, if they were all over the map, you can say, "Thanks so much for sharing; you mentioned x, y, and z. Which one is your top priority?" This helps your prospect focus. Question two helps your prospect elaborate, providing additional details that are top of mind for them and their business. Remember, **people don't just need your service, they need a trusted guide who can help them make a positive change**. If you can't help them get to the root cause of what's happening and what's important, why should they work with you at all?

Questions one and two kick off a focused conversation, allowing your prospect to hone in on what matters to them. It's important to steer clear of general business operations (e.g., tell me about your business). This is too broad. Your prospect may be all too happy to talk about the ins and outs of their systems, infrastructure, and history. While interesting, you will want to guide them toward the problems that need solving; that's where you can help. They may tell you that they can't get their sales engine going, or that their employees keep quitting, or there are operational inefficiencies. Your next question is just as simple as the previous:

3. How long has this been happening?: What this third question does is to begin to qualify your prospect's situation. Asking, "How long has this been happening?" helps your prospect reflect and consider the impact of their situation over a period of time. Remember, many prospects are stuck. They may be fixated on current events or the immediate issue at hand. Asking about time helps solidify what's important to your prospect. It helps to quantify the business impact of their situation.

The nice thing about question three is that it leads really well into question four. That is, by reflecting on time, your prospect can draw on a number of key moments, decisions, and changes that may have contributed to their current reality. As with the others, the simplicity of question four should not be underestimated.

4. What have you tried, and how did it work?: Number four can be asked this way - "You're obviously a seasoned executive and have been doing this awhile. What have you tried, and how did it work?" This allows your prospect to think about their efforts, what worked, what didn't, and how much time and resources were spent on trying to address their situation. This question helps unpack business context. It can get competitive solutions out on the table and help you get clear on what matters to your prospect.

Allowing your prospect to reflect on their efforts helps them to gain clarity. It can help them begin to think about other possibilities, too. This brings us to question five.

5. What's the business impact?: This question might sound like this. "Help me understand how this is impacting your business, economically or otherwise." This opens the door for your prospect to expand on the ramifications of their particular situation. Importantly, it's not always directly money, although that's typically the big one. Other impacts could be employee morale, productivity, Glassdoor reviews, brand, or customer satisfaction scores. This is a critical step that's important to helping your prospect quantify their situation. It will help them to see the economic realities of the status quo. Sometimes your prospect will be comfortable with the status quo - or stuck in a status quo mindset. By helping them put a number to their situation, you can help them get unstuck.

This last question helps your prospect weigh the particular situation you uncovered against all the other competing priorities they may have.

6. Where does this land on your priority list?: This last question gets to why this matters to your prospect at a personal level. It can help your prospect understand why they care and why this is important to them. It sounds like this: "You obviously have a lot on your plate. Where does solving this situation land on your list of priorities on a scale of one to ten - one being top priority, ten being not important at all?" You can follow up with, "Why would you put it there?" And finally, "Are there any other reasons why?" And even, "I appreciate that, anything else?" These last questions help to unlock areas that a prospect may have yet to voice, allowing you to really hone in on what matters to them and focus there.

To understand the power of this prioritization question and the follow-up questions, let me share an example. I asked a prospect four times if there were any other reasons why she ranked her situation at number one. Each time she added a new concern: her board was worried, she was unsure of her own leadership, a new COO was coming on board, and she was afraid for her own job if she didn't rectify the situation we had discussed. These four items came to light after we had already spent forty-five minutes discussing her most serious business challenges. This woman was in a lot of pain. While hard, it felt good to help her get clear on what she needed to do to move forward in a positive direction.

Answering these questions can be therapeutic for your prospects. They often do not get a chance to talk about what's really going on under the surface. They're in the fray, reacting instead of taking the time to think things through. They may not have a safe environment in which to open up. Helping your prospect think through their situation at a deeper level is valuable guidance in itself.

Importantly, the point of these questions is to let your prospect talk. Too often, salespeople don't actually take the time to listen. These questions require active listening. As you wrap up your questions, there's a critical step that's often missed - a recap.

Recap

It can be tempting to take what your prospect has told you and jump straight to solutions. This is normal; you want to help. However, your prospect has likely experienced a bit of an emotional roller coaster ride, discussing the difficulties with their situation. It's important that they know you've heard them. Imagine, for example, that your spouse came home after getting into a fender bender. You run out to the driveway and say, "Don't worry, we'll get this fixed up in no time. I'll take it to the body shop and get it looking brand new again!" How will your spouse feel? Unheard.

Similar to the unpleasant feelings triggered by reactance, if a prospect doesn't feel heard and understood, they'll lose trust in you as their guide. Have you ever been working out a problem with someone (a boss, friend, or spouse) and they essentially announce, "Got it," and then proceed to check out of the conversation even though you're still talking? It happens all the time in everyday life. It happens in sales, too. A salesperson thinks they've understood the prospect's core need and so launches into presentation mode. Meanwhile, the prospect is feeling slighted, misunderstood, and not validated.

A better approach is to recap what you've heard. Here's an example:

"I appreciate what you've shared with me, helping me to get a better understanding of you and your situation. Could I take a minute and give it back to you to ensure I've heard you right?

So, for the past year, your sales numbers have been off. Certainly the economy hasn't helped and the competition is picking up, but in your case, you've identified that your marketing and sales teams are not working together effectively, which is confusing your clients. You estimate this is costing the business roughly two million annually, but it's also impacting morale and engagement with your employees, as well as customer satisfaction ratings. In terms of priority, this ranks number one for you, and you'd like to turn this around ASAP. Did I get that right? What did I miss?"

This recap lets your prospect know you've been listening and that you understand what's at stake. They will feel heard. Moreover, by asking, "What did I miss?" at the end, you create safety, allowing your prospect to correct you and fill in any gaps. At the same time, your prospect may want to add and/or clarify something that they may have missed.

At this point, you're ready to transition to part two of the discovery conversation - potential solutions. This is less about a shift to presenting a solution, although that may be appropriate. Rather, this is a shift to understand how to best help your prospect. Depending on your services and/or industry, a demo may be appropriate, or there may be a need for additional conversations, or it may be to review a proposal together. Whatever the context, simplicity and clarity is key. I'll flesh out an example in a subsequent chapter, but for now, let's look at an overview of part two of Exploring.

Part Two: Potential Solutions

There are three parts to this section:
1. Solution discussion
2. Next steps
3. Confirm plan

Solution Discussion

This is where you explore solutions, both their ideal solution, and the unique value you bring to the table to solve their problem. Keep it simple. Too often, this is where your prospect gets confused. Consider the power of three. For example, you might say, "Based on our discussion, there are three steps we can take to approach what we just discussed…"

Breaking your solution into three steps allows your prospect to absorb the information, and see the path ahead. Prospects get nervous when there isn't clear guidance. Showing the steps to success de-risks things for your prospect. The principles at play here are safety, clarity, and simplicity.

Next Steps

As you discuss potential solutions and lay out the best way to solve your prospect's concerns, the next steps need to be clear. This is where many deals fall apart because there is no clear plan forward nor an understanding of how to best work within your prospect's context. You'll see how to do this in depth in chapter twelve. For now, an understanding of timing, internal purchasing dynamics, and who's involved is critical to helping your prospect decide to work with you.

Confirm Plan

Lastly, it's important to confirm the plan. Whether that plan is another conversation, demo, or signature, an email that lays out clear next steps is appreciated by busy prospects, who, after meeting with you, may be inundated with any number of issues. There's an email example ahead you can adapt to your context.

To put this discovery approach all together, here's an example of a real conversation (modified for privacy), that I had with a prospect. You'll see me navigate part one. We'll do a deeper dive on part two in chapter twelve:

Part One:
1. A simple opener
2. Six follow up questions
3. Recap & transition

A Simple Opener

Me: I'm not sure this is on your mind, but when I talk with other executives, they tell me that they're wrestling with the changes of rightsizing, operating lean, and shuffling priorities. Some are concerned about the negative impacts on their culture, which may be impacting productivity and brand. And some are concerned about how to rebound well from the troubling economy.

Is any of this your experience, or have I missed the mark?

Prospect: No, no, that is certainly top of mind - I've got tension on my executive team, and low Glassdoor ratings are hurting us. We're losing business to competitors. Our brand and reputation are suffering, and customer complaints are up. I'm most concerned the company is not all on the same page anymore, especially with the new direction we're taking.

Tell me more

Me: That sounds like a full plate, tell me more about the new direction…

Prospect: Sure, yeah, we've had to pivot our strategy really fast, moving from an inbound sales model that is very process driven to an outbound sales model to rent our storage space. Our sales team is not doing well at all. Revenue has dropped by 40%, and we're not making a lot of headway to rent out our storage facilities.

Specifics & Examples

Me: I appreciate you sharing that with me. Are there any other specifics, or a recent example of this? How's this playing out in your context?

Prospect: Yeah, good question. I'm not sure we have the right sales team in place. They seem to lack the drive and ambition you'd expect. Just the other day our VP of sales said that some on the team don't want to pick up the phone.

How long

Me: How long has this been happening?

Prospect: Definitely since last April. They do well with inbound leads. They're great at planning, logistics, and running the process from A to Z, but they're floundering now in terms of generating new business with the shift to outbound.

What have you tried

Me: You've been doing this a long time. You know the business well. What have you tried, and how did it work?

Prospect: I've mostly been working with our sales VP to see what we can do. She's essentially just as frustrated. She's pushing the team pretty hard, trying to incentivize, write a new playbook, and get them going. Nothing has moved the needle.

Business impact

Me: Got it. Help me understand what's at risk here. You mentioned a 40% drop in revenue - what does that mean in terms of business impact, and are there other costs associated with this?

Prospect: For sure, we're talking at least a loss of one million annually in terms of net new business. If things continue, it may mean more layoffs, more belt-tightening - and we've already done quite a bit. Morale is fairly low, too.

Where does land on your priority list

Me: I hear you. I can certainly appreciate that. Now, you're obviously busy, spinning a lot of plates. On a scale of one to ten, where does addressing your sales team's performance land on your priority list?

Prospect: It's definitely number one! It's front and center! We need to get this sales engine humming ASAP. Secondly, we need to get engagement up.

Me: Are there any other reasons why this is front and center for you?

Prospect: Well, yeah, I mean, I've got a legacy here. We've been doing this for 40 years. I don't want to be the one at the helm when the ship sinks. I care about the livelihoods of our people and our customers.

Me: I hear that - anything else?

Prospect: Hmm, well, if I'm being honest, I may not be leading as effectively as I could be. Maybe I've moved too fast and alienated some on my team. I know I haven't communicated as effectively as I could. In short, there's a lot at stake and I'm looking for some fast solutions to right the ship.

Me: I appreciate that. Thanks for sharing with me. Would it be okay if I summarized what I heard to ensure I didn't miss anything?

Prospect: Of course, please do.

Recap

Me: You started by talking about some executive tension and some brand and reputation concerns. But what's top of mind for you is the new outbound initiative with your sales team to drive revenue. You've been working hard with your VP to coach and incentivize the sales team, but they haven't responded in a way that is driving the results needed. The impact to the business is one million dollars in net new revenue, and there are concerns around morale, engagement, and the potential for more belt-tightening. You're also looking to ensure that you're leading effectively through these difficult times. Ideally, you're hoping for some quick wins to get things moving in the right direction and boost morale. Is that an accurate picture of what you told me? What did I miss?

Prospect: No, you didn't miss anything. You got it.

* * *

How did this part of the conversation feel to you? Did it feel high pressure, or did it feel natural? I can tell you that when I do this live with clients, they appreciate it. They feel like someone has actually heard them. Some even say it's therapeutic. Folks I train say they appreciate how organic it is. It doesn't feel forced. It feels good.

To be clear, these aren't the only questions you can ask, but they are effective - and they're easy to adopt. Also, things may come up in your conversation that are outside of your capabilities. That's okay. You can recap their situation and ask if any of the things that you cannot do are a deal breaker. They rarely are. Even if they are, it's better to know early so you can move on to help someone who needs your services.

After all these questions, you may be thinking, what if the buyer doesn't want to be asked a bunch of questions? It's a fair point because it's true! Some people just want to see what you have. Here are three things to consider:

1. If someone is not willing to engage in a business conversation, you may not have a real buyer. They may just be kicking the tires. If so, you can feel good about parting as friends and saving valuable time. Be careful though. Expectations have changed. Buyers expect speed. Having grown up on computers, apps and a host of try-before-you-buy products, your prospect may already be far along their buying journey and just want to see how you compare. This is okay. Adjust your process accordingly, or consider the Rapid Discovery process below.

2. Perhaps you didn't set the stage for a business conversation, but instead laid out a path to show features and benefits. This isn't necessarily bad. It just depends on the expectations you

want to set with your prospect, as well as what works best in your context.

3. You can always ask your questions as you go. That is you can jump into a solution conversation or product demo, asking questions as you go, like, What's top of mind for you? Or, to ensure we focus on what's most important to you, where should we start?

***

We've spent a good amount of time reviewing part one of the classic discovery process. Again, you'll see more of part two in chapter twelve under Presenting. You'll discover how you can help your prospects get to the finish line with you.

As we turn to the Rapid Discovery approach, there are similarities to the classic discovery process. However, it may have some advantages depending on your context.

Rapid Discovery

Discovery is a sacred cow in sales. There are purists who demand a full discovery. Then there are pragmatists, like me, who see the new reality of selling. This is why I created Rapid Discovery. It allows for flexibility and to hone in on what matters most to your prospect quickly and efficiently. To do the Rapid Discovery approach well, you need to do your homework. In sales, this is called pre-call planning. This doesn't need to be a massive undertaking with hours of research - fifteen to thirty minutes should suffice. I typically add it as an agenda item in my sales conversations. It sounds something like this, "I'd like to take a minute to confirm what I know about you and your organization; would that be okay?" Everyone agrees to this because it's all about them - as it should be. Here's a real-life example, adapted for privacy.

"Great, let's jump in. Here's what I know. XYZ Corp is a leader in pricing SaaS software solutions. You're located in Chicago. You have approximately 250 employees. Your organization was just awarded the Top 150 Fastest Growing Companies - congratulations! You have risen in the ranks and are now the VP of HR. You have been there 4 years. My understanding from your initial inquiry is that you're looking to revitalize your marketing team. There's some concern about bias in your hiring process so you're exploring options to address this. Your mission is to grow the business 2X in the next 3 years. Is this accurate? What did I miss?"

How do you think this type of approach lands with a prospect? The most common response is a smile of appreciation along with, "You've got it!" Sometimes, you'll even get a job offer.

What this approach does is help your prospect feel like they're talking to someone who knows, which will help them to feel safe and heard. You are instantly seen as someone worth talking to.

You'll notice that I told the prospect's story. I started at a high level with the company and then moved to the individual. I then highlighted the problem that they're looking to solve and where they want to go as an organization.

This rapid discovery approach can open the door to a great discussion around their main concern. Just like with classic discovery, you'll want to recap before transitioning to presenting solutions. Here's an example. Notice the additional details:

"So, if I'm hearing you right, the turnover is impacting your sales revenue by six figures every quarter. It's number one on your list of priorities to address. Is there anything else you want to add, or should we switch gears and talk a little bit about how we approach situations like yours?"

The above conversation can be completed in under ten minutes, or it may go on for longer if your prospect has a lot on their mind. If so, let them talk. Whether you're using classic or rapid discovery, both require a safe environment for your prospect in order to have a great conversation to help your prospect find their way.

* * *

The key principles at play in the Exploring step can be boiled down to what I call: Pain, Power, and a Plan (PPP).

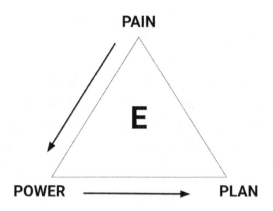

Pain - Pain is what you uncover when you are exploring. Or, it's what's most important to your prospect. This is the dragon you are helping your prospect to slay. The problem is identified, quantified, and prioritized so you can provide a solution.

Power - Power refers to the individual you are talking to. You want to be talking to people who can get things done. For example, if you're talking to an owner of an organization, they'll likely have a lot of power to purchase your services. However, if you're talking to a low-level manager at a company, they may not have the power to move things forward. To be clear, power is not necessarily related to title. While it's always great to have the ear of the c-suite, power is anyone who sees you as a solution and is willing to help you navigate the organization so they can use your services. Additionally, there are often multiple people involved in purchase decisions.

Plan - The plan refers to setting up next steps. Too often, sales conversations end with non-commitment and promises to follow up. This doesn't feel good. Instead, the plan helps you best help your prospect get to where they want to go.

These three principles also act as a diagnostic tool for any deals that may have stalled or gone bad for you.

Deals go bad for these three primary reasons:

1. Unclear pain: When your prospect's problem has not clearly been identified, quantified, and prioritized, the commercial value of your services is less clear.

2. No power: When you're talking to the wrong person, deals can't move forward. They may be happy to chat with you, but they don't have the power to get a deal done.

3. Vague plan: When prospects are not invited into taking clear next steps forward, deals fall apart. When the plan forward is vague it opens the door to distractions. People get busy, and your services get pushed off.

Here's a visual of the Exploring movement followed by a summary of the key principles for you to keep in mind:

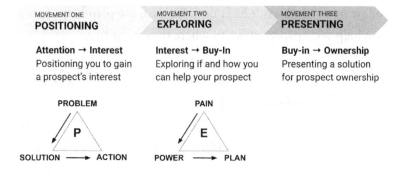

Summary of key principles with Exploring (PPP):

1. **PAIN**: Create a safe environment to get under the surface to address business problems

2. **POWER**: Conduct conversations with the right people to move a deal forward

3. **PLAN**: Guide and invite your prospect with a clear plan forward to address their needs

Regardless of which approach you take or emphasize - classic or rapid discovery - there is a critical component to consider: creating a safe environment. You'll see how you can create a safe environment for your prospects in the next chapter.

Chapter 10

Creating a Safe Environment

If there's one sales skill that is in desperate short supply, it is the ability to create a safe environment. That is, does your prospect feel safe with you? This can make or break your deal. Many sales conversations fall apart because the salesperson is making the prospect feel uncomfortable. Sometimes it's a blatant sales tactic, other times it's a poor choice of words. In this chapter, you'll see how you can avoid this, and create an environment of safety to have good conversations with your prospects.

The simplest way to do this is to set the stage at the outset with an agenda. This allows the prospect to feel safe and the salesperson to effectively lead. I will outline a four-part agenda that leads to a great sales conversation.

4-Part Agenda

1. Setting the tone and expectations
2. Getting permission to ask questions
3. Introducing your unique approach
4. Guiding the path forward to an outcome

It only takes your prospect a few minutes to identify your level of planning and professionalism. Therefore, it is essential to set the right tone, letting your prospect see that you are a trusted guide to help them move from point A to point B. They want to feel safe with you. You can use this simple agenda to set up, guide, and end your sales conversations in a way that is professional, respectful, effective, and safe.

Doing this well requires a plan. Many salespeople try to wing it, thinking on their feet and/or using wit or charm. This rarely lands well with prospects. Other salespeople get overly excited. They talk for too long, and focus too much on themselves. On the opposite end, some people put so much structure in place they provide no breathing room for the prospect. Like Tommy Callahan in the movie *Tommy Boy* they hold on so tightly, trying so hard, that they interrupt their prospects, confuse them, and wind up setting their model car on fire. Lack of a good plan does not inspire confidence in your prospects.

Let's look more closely at this 4-part agenda framework.

Setting the tone and expectations

One of my sales mentors was asked during a training session, "What's the first question you ask a prospect?" His answer surprised everyone. He paused and said, "Do we still have the hour?"

People were confused. What was my mentor saying? He was saying that in order to have a good sales conversation, you need to set the boundaries, starting at the most basic expectation: time. Many skip this, but time is the most obvious and important expectation. Starting the conversation with, "I have an hour set aside on my calendar; does that still work for you?" sets the tone and expectations in at least three ways.

1. There has been agreement to a meeting. Your prospect made a commitment and so did you. By starting with time, you're reconfirming that commitment. Boundaries create safety.

2. This is a serious business conversation, not a friendly chat. You will need this time to explore what's most important to your prospect so you can most effectively help.

3. Everyone's time is valuable, including yours. This is a peer-to-peer conversation. Your time as a salesperson is very valuable, and you are bringing value to the table.

Too often, salespeople set a tone of weakness instead of leadership, saying, "Oh, thank you so much Mrs. Prospect for taking the time to speak with me. I really appreciate it. We may not even need the full hour." This type of submissive behavior sends the message that they're doing you a favor to talk with you. This doesn't feel good. The salesperson is essentially abdicating their responsibility as a trusted guide. This will not create safety. The good news is that this can be fixed easily by leading with a time expectation when you sit down to talk with your prospect. Whatever your time frame, start by confirming it. It's true. It's respectful. It's professional. It's safe. It feels good.

Getting permission to ask questions

The second part of the agenda is to get permission from the prospect to learn about them and their business. Too often, salespeople just jump in and start asking questions, many of which are uncomfortable to the prospect. Rather than getting under the surface to root issues, the prospect starts to feel defensive. They literally clam up. To create a safe environment that allows you to identify what's important to your prospect, you will need to get your prospect's permission. Prospects may be super passionate about their company, beaming with pride, or they may be deeply frustrated that things are not going well. Either way, asking for permission up front to learn about them shows that you respect them, that you care enough to learn, and that this is a safe space.

It sounds something like this, "To ensure that I understand you and your situation, I'd like to ask you some questions. Would that be okay with you?" If you're using the rapid discovery approach, you can change it to, "To ensure that I understand you and your situation, I'd like to take a minute to clarify what I know so far. Would that be okay with you?" Wait for your prospect to answer. The answer is always a resounding yes. Why? Because you've shown that you care enough to learn about their business. By asking, you create safety.

Introducing your unique approach

Introducing your unique approach is not an opportunity to talk about how awesome you are. Rather, it's an opportunity to solidify a safe environment.

It might sound something like this: "To be clear, our approach isn't for everyone. Unlike standard solutions, we take a different tact. Would it be alright if I spent a few minutes outlining some of this to see whether or not it's for you?" The answer is always yes. Why? Wouldn't you want to see a unique approach that could help you? Additionally, there's no pressure. It's simply an invitation to see if something will work for the prospect or not. It's safe.

This puts your prospect at ease. It places the responsibility to decide where it belongs - on your prospect. This creates safety. With these steps in place, the salesperson can now suggest an outcome.

Guiding the path forward to an outcome

To be a trusted guide, you need to lead, not force, your prospects to an outcome. You do this by building the outcome into the agenda on the front end. When salespeople fail to do this the outcomes are muddy and often end with a non-committal, "I'll follow up with you," or, "Thanks, we'll let you know." This is a clear indicator that the salesperson missed a step. To avoid this, build the outcome into your agenda. It might sound something like this: "Lastly, provided what we discuss today resonates with you, could we use the last ten minutes of our time to explore next steps together?" Prospects always agree to this. Why? The salesperson has created a safe environment. They have set boundaries and asked permission. They have made no assumptions that their solution is the be-all and end-all. The next steps are contingent on the prospect's interest. Obviously, if they like what they see, they will be willing to discuss next steps. If not, they already have permission to bail. This feels good and sets the stage for a great conversation.

You can seamlessly add an agenda to your sales conversations. Here's an example of what it might sound like.

"I have an hour on my calendar; does that still work for you? Good. I'd first like to ensure I understand you and your situation. Would it be okay if I asked you some questions? Thanks. Now, our approach is a little different, and it isn't for everyone, but I'd like to cover some things at a high level as they relate to you and your context; would that be okay? Great. Finally, and only if what we discuss today resonates with you, would it be okay if we spend the last ten minutes of our time exploring next steps together - does this sound like a good use of our time?

The answer is almost always, yes, to every one of these questions because they are geared to create an environment of safety.

With this brief backdrop, you'll see this idea of creating a safe environment repeated as we move into Presenting.

PART FOUR

PRESENTING
Presenting For Ownership

Chapter 11

How to Present a Solution So That Your Prospect Owns It

How do you present a solution so your prospects say:

- I can see this helping my business.
- I really like this, can I use it here, too?
- Yes, I love this, let's do it!

How do you do it in a way that honors your prospect's journey and doesn't manipulate them? To do this well, there are three core elements to consider.

1. Story. You must tell your prospect's story. What is most important to them? What are you going to help them solve? Don't go off that script. Avoid the traditional features and benefits approach that many salespeople run through during their demos and presentations. Your prospect cares about solving *their* problem - *their* story. You need to tie their most important pain (or the thing most important to them) directly to your solution.

2. Vision. Cast a vision of what's possible if your prospect should decide to work with you. You want to help your prospect see what life would be like, and what they would have the ability to do if they worked with you. Many sales presentations are lectures on *how* to do something. Lectures are boring. Instead of showing them how to do something, paint a picture of their future state and the new abilities they would have.

3. Ownership. Position your language and approach in such a way as to let your prospect take ownership. This is a tough mindshift for some. Instead of the traditional sales questions that attempt to force a yes, you'll see how you can invite your prospect to say yes by asking better questions. If this seems obvious, it is. Yet, in practice, it's rare.

Let's look at these three core elements more closely.

Telling Their Story

It is essential to tell your prospect's lead story. If you recall, in the example of the struggling sales team from chapter nine, the prospect's main concern was that their sales team wasn't delivering the results they needed. There were several other concerns, too: morale, competition, brand, and even leadership development. However, the main concern was the sales team. That was their lead story. It was what was most important to them at that point in time. There may be other stories (sub plots), but these are secondary. The key is addressing the lead story.

Speaking of stories, let me tell you one to drive home the importance of **telling their story**.

I once asked a landscaper to give me a price to put some shrubs in my front yard. The request was simple enough. My yard was a mess. With four kids and two dogs it needed a lot of work. The landscaper took a look and promised to provide an estimate. A couple of days later, he provided me with an estimate to do a spring clean up. To be fair, the yard certainly needed a spring cleaning. I thanked him for the estimate and asked, "What about the shrubs?" He replied, "Oh, yeah, I'll need to get back to you on that."

Do you think he got the job?

No way.

He didn't address my lead story. There was a lot this landscaper didn't understand about my primary pain point. For example, I was perfectly fine with a messy yard. In fact, the mess was intentional. I want my kids running around, playing in the dirt, making forts, and so on. I was also perfectly comfortable putting four rakes into their hands and cleaning up the yard ourselves. What I did not know how to do was plant shrubs. I didn't know the names of shrubs. I didn't know where to plant them or how far from the house they should be set. I didn't know which ones needed sun, and which ones preferred shade. I didn't know how much water they needed and when. If the landscaper had helped me solve *my lead story*, I would have hired him on the spot.

So, when you present your solution, it's important to put your finger on your prospect's most important item and address that first. A simple way to ensure that you nail this is by placing a recap section in your presentation agenda. The good news is you don't need a whole new agenda format, you only need to add a recap section to your agenda when you're presenting. It's very simple and sounds like this. "To ensure I've captured everything, I'd like to spend a couple minutes reviewing our previous conversation to make sure I haven't missed anything; would that be okay?" Everyone agrees to this. It shows that you care to get it right. It also allows for any gaps or changes to be discussed since your last conversation. Finally, it serves to remind your prospect that there are serious business concerns at stake. In the case of the sales example I shared above, it would sound like this:

"Last time we talked, we discussed how the economic downturn caused you to course correct with a new initiative and a new direction for your sales team. The sales team hasn't responded in a way that is driving the results needed for the business. The impact to the business is one million dollars in net new revenue, and there are concerns around morale and engagement. Has anything changed since our last conversation? What would you add?"

This little recap will ensure you hit the nail on the head for your prospect. Most will say, "You've got it." But what if, since your last meeting, your prospect's focus had shifted to leadership concerns? Imagine what would happen if you plowed ahead with your presentation in light of this change in priority?

Sometimes a new member of your prospect's team shows up for the presentation. They may have something they want to emphasize. This is perfectly okay. If it's clear this is a new and important direction, you may need to back up and ask some discovery questions, e.g., "I'm glad you brought that up. Tell me more." In the sales team example, you might say, "I'm glad to hear you say that leadership is top of mind. Should we address that first, or explore the situation with the sales team first and then circle back?" You can then adjust your presentation to highlight the areas that are important to your audience while staying focused on their lead story.

What do you think your prospect's response will be if you miss their lead story? It's one of the most common (and misunderstood) responses in sales. Perhaps you've heard it once or twice. Your prospect will state a polite, "That's interesting." Cue that epic fail sound in your head, wa, wa, wa. Surprisingly, the annoyingly over-excited salespeople that irk you take this response as a positive. They say something like, "I know, right!," and keep droning on. Here's what they don't realize:

"That's interesting" does not equal an engaged prospect. It doesn't rule it out, of course, but it's not a great indicator. Good indicators are responses such as, "I can see us using this," or, "This would be great to roll out at our all-company meeting," or, "Could this also be used with this other situation?"

Sadly, in most cases, a "that's interesting" response is related to the fact that the salesperson is not hitting the core pain and motivating needs of the prospect. However, there is a caveat to the "interesting" response. Occasionally, the prospect uses this phrase to indicate they are truly learning something. You have helped them to see something in a new light, or you've expanded their worldview in some way. Fantastic; keep doing this! Just be sure you recognize the difference between genuine interest and polite dismissal.

Casting vision

When helping your hero, you'll want to cast a vision of what they will have the ability to do with your product or service. Show them what's possible before going into details. What arrows will you add to their quiver? What tools will you add to their toolbelt? This is starting with the end in mind, and it is critical. Suppose you gave a presentation to the population of a dilapidated city that proposed rebuilding the entire city. If you started with the step-by-step details, blueprints, and costs, you'd lose them, right? They wouldn't be able to envision what you already see. Instead, you might say, "Imagine our city with tree-lined streets, graffiti-free buildings, a fenced-in park with a duck pond and a child-safe play area." See the difference? Your prospects need to see where they're going. You need to cast vision.

Here's an example from the prospect with the struggling sales team:

"Before we dive into specifics, I'd like to show you the end result that we're hoping to achieve with your sales team. Imagine having the ability to understand your team in such a way as to allow you to pinpoint not only what's wrong, but where your team needs coaching, and which strengths they have that you can double down on to drive the results you're looking for with your new initiative. In concert with your VP of sales, we'd use data and analytics to get this team hitting its goals, working well together, and rapidly closing the one million dollar gap. The process is called Sales Power Up. It provides you and your team the ability to identify, track, and improve your team's sales performance through sales metrics and behavioral change. Unlike other solutions that focus on one or the other, Sales Power Up allows you to address both the people-side of your business and the sales numbers. A simple interface allows you to see talent strengths and gaps, and the sales dashboards enable you to track performance at a glance. Now before I go too far, how this resonating with you, or is this not what you had in mind?"

Did you notice where I started? I started with the end in mind. I made sure to cast a vision for the prospect so they could see where I was taking them. Simple words like "imagine" and "picture" help your potential clients see what the world might be like if they were to work with you. This isn't a sales technique. It's a fundamental human need for hope. It feels good to provide hope. We all want to be successful. We all want a better life, a better way of doing business, and a better future. In this case, it's a struggling sales team, who, up to this point, probably just feels yelled at. If you're going to be a trusted guide, learning to help your prospect step into the future with your services is key.

It's also essential to emphasize the *ability to*. Using language such as "ability to," "enables you to," or, "allows you to," accomplishes two things. Most importantly, it allows your prospect to enter the story. It allows them to see what you would be arming them with to go and fight their battle. Secondly, these words help you to focus on their specific situation. That is, they have pain, a challenge. They want to overcome that challenge. You are there to say, "Here's what you **will be able** to do if we work together." Rather than showing them all kinds of features and functionality, if you focus on the *ability to*, you'll provide clear value to your prospect.

Once you've cast the vision, you can get into specific features that unpack more abilities. For example, you might say, "You mentioned that your VP of sales has been working hard with the team. The good news is, with the Sales Power Up program, you're able to utilize the virtual sales training that's included. These weekly one-hour sessions enable your sales team to uncover their natural strengths, and identify any blind spots that may be limiting their performance, such as not wanting to pick up the phone as you mentioned. There's also a separate sales leadership course that would allow your VP to gain deep insights into each member on the sales team. With the insights from these sessions, your VP can coach in a more targeted manner. This will save time and have a faster impact on the team. Does this sound like it might be helpful in your context, or not so much?"

Do you see how everything in this example is tied back to the core concern of getting the sales team humming? It doesn't matter what your particular service is, everything you talk about, show, feature or highlight should tie back to the prospect's lead story.

Of course, there are exceptions. It may be that your product or service does something in a unique way, requiring your prospect to think differently about the situation. Great. You can use contrast and reframe as discussed earlier. Here is an example of using contrast and reframe in the sales team example:

"As mentioned, our approach isn't for everyone. Unlike most solutions that tend to force one sales methodology on an unwilling team, we take a strategic approach. You're able to draw on the unique strengths within your existing sales team and process. In this way, you're empowered to make targeted modifications that have a big impact instead of disruptive wholesale change. The last thing we want to do is slow you down. Rather, the goal would be to get you some quick wins and set a path that achieves the goals you're after with what we call Mod Training. The Mod Training allows you not only to identify and modify specific areas of the sales team that are not functioning well, but it is also a modular approach that enables faster learning with step-by-step modules for you and your team. Does this seem like it would be a fit, or have I drifted off course?"

Offering something that a prospect didn't ask for is perfectly fine as long as it pertains to one of their core concerns. You are the solutions expert. You are the one who spends time helping people fix problems. If it doesn't pertain to their core concerns, you're wasting your breath. You will also minimize the value of what does address your prospect's main concern. Less is definitely more if you're not adding direct value.

Ownership

At this point, you have addressed your prospect's lead story and you have emphasized the abilities they would have to address their concern. The ownership questions used during and at the end of your presentation put the decision making right where it belongs: with your prospect. No matter how well you think you landed a particular point or how well you think you can read people, you do not know what the prospect is thinking. Rather than guessing or assuming, you must ask. This seems like a fairly obvious point, right? The stunning reality, and one of the reasons why you may not feel good about selling, is that most sales questions are really bad. The questions are typically leading, manipulative, lazy, intrusive, or rude.

Did you notice the ownership questions I asked the prospect during the presentation? Each one was designed to provide the prospect the freedom to choose and to correct me. This is their decision - not mine.

I asked three ownership questions:

1. Now before I go too far, how is this resonating with you, or is this not what you had in mind?"

2. Does this sound like it might be helpful in your context, or not so much?"

3. Does this seem like it would be a fit, or have I drifted off course?"

Other ownership questions during the presenting stage can be just as helpful to your prospect. For example, "How is this resonating with you so far, or does it not quite scratch the itch?" One of my favorites is, "Is this what you had in mind, or am I barking up the wrong tree?" Your prospect may laugh and say, "No, this is exactly what I was hoping for!"

Asking about feelings can also help your prospect find their way; for example, "How are you feeling about this as a potential solution? Is it resonating or not so much?" With these types of questions, there is total freedom for your prospect. They can engage, ask questions, discover additional insights, and, of course, **take ownership for their decision**.

As you work through your prospect's story, helping them to feel safe, envisioning a new future, and taking ownership of it, there is one thing you must avoid at all costs: asking bad questions.

Below is a list of seven questions that are common and that you'll want to eliminate from your vocabulary. For each bad question, I'll suggest an alternative you can adapt to your context.

Seven questions you should never ask:

1. Any questions? This question doesn't do what the question intends. The intention is to find out if something is resonating (or not) with your prospect. A better approach is to simply ask, "How is this resonating with you, or am I off track?" This is a more authentic question that invites participation and ownership of the journey from your prospect. It also helps to keep your prospect engaged, and lets them know this is a safe place for them to speak up.

2. What questions do you have about this? This may sound better. It's not. While it can invite some participation, it's also assumptive. Assuming can irritate your prospect. This question can also be answered by your prospect with, "none," which is less than helpful. A more honest and engaging question is, "Let me pause here. In what ways is this in line with what you were thinking, or is it missing the mark?

3. Does that make sense? What if it doesn't make sense to your prospect? How do you think they might feel? Good? Probably not. Asking this question risks putting your prospect in the awkward position of not knowing. This is not going to create a safe environment for them. Just eliminate the question. Instead, ask, "I've just shown you a lot; does this seem like it would address what we've discussed, or not so much? Or, "I've shown you a lot; how is this resonating with you, or is this not what you had in mind?"

4. What are your pain points and challenges? This question can quickly trip psychological reactance. You may have a prospect respond with, "I wouldn't call them pain points or challenges!" Why are they saying this? You've put them in a vulnerable position. They are now on the defensive. A safer question is, "When I talk with others like yourself, they tell me that they're wrestling with X, Y, and Z. Is this your experience, or am I off base?"

5. Why is this a priority? This risks creating doubt. Your prospect may doubt the seriousness of their situation and/or your solution. A better and more respectful way to ask is, "Where does addressing this situation land on your priority scale?" This provides your prospect the freedom and safety to quantify their situation.

6. Tell me about your business? You should already know a lot about your prospect's business. Pre-call planning and a simple opener (discussed earlier) is a far better way of showing that you're someone worth talking to. For example, "When I talk with other professionals like you who want to avoid annoying sales techniques, they tell me that they're uncomfortable manipulating people or pressuring them. Sometimes they're simply at a loss for the words to say in order to sell. For others, even the thought of sales makes them anxious. At the same time, these folks are sincere and passionate about what they do. They want to help people address a real need, but they feel like they don't know where to start. Is any of this on your mind, or am I way out in left field?" See the difference?

7. If I could, would you…? What if I told you…? These sentences are a form of manipulation. The salesperson is trying to leverage transactional techniques to apply pressure. A sense of urgency isn't always bad, especially when trying to nudge a deal forward, but a better approach is to be honest and say something like, "I'm not sure this would help you, but sometimes I include a one-time incentive with two-year agreements. Is this of interest, or should we stick with one year?" In this example, there's no pressure. Rather, this puts the decision into the hands of the prospect to take advantage of your incentive or not.

As an aside, be careful when it comes to offering discounts to your product and/or services. Likewise, avoid offering incentives, extras, payment plans, and more to get a deal closed. This devalues your product and services. Question number seven allows you to probe in areas that might be of interest to your prospect. If you hit the right area, you may be able to begin working with your prospect sooner versus later. But be careful. I once told a prospect I could save him some money if he purchased my services this month. He told me his issue wasn't the money, it was his time. I worked out a solution to address his time concerns and I won a new client. However, because I had offered a discount, too, I had to extend that as well. Use incentives sparingly and be sure to find out what matters to your prospect first.

***

Avoiding bad questions is a great start. It's also important to avoid bad words. No, I'm not talking about swear words. Rather, there are certain words that can trigger a negative reaction in your prospects. When you are talking to your prospects, it's important to remember that you are dealing with problems and pain. *Pain* is a trigger word that can trip psychological reactance. While you do need to talk about *pain*, your prospect will likely feel more comfortable if you use a different word.

Words like *pain*, *challenges*, *issues*, and *problems*, can produce defensive responses from prospects. Here are three examples with common trigger words:

1. Salesperson: "So what's the problem you're wrestling with most?"

Prospect: "Well, I don't know if it's a *problem*. I mean, there are always ups and downs."

2. Salesperson: "It sounds like there are a number of challenges at play."

Prospect: "I don't know if I'd go so far as to call them *challenges*. We're working hard and making good progress."

3. Salesperson: "So what are your pain points and biggest issues you're having?"

Prospect: "I don't think I'd call them *pain points* or *issues*, but rather we need a little help navigating some changes."

Notice how the prospects reacted. They got defensive. These words are so common in sales that it's easy to overlook the damage they're causing. Why are they so damaging? It makes your prospect feel bad. It makes them feel like they're doing something wrong. These are primal emotions. They are deep down and usually unexpressed. Yet they are always felt by your prospect. People do not like to have pain, problems, challenges, and issues. Whether consciously or unconsciously, these words risk hurting your prospects and your deals.

Here's a simple chart with some replacement words that are safer and more respectful to your prospect's journey.

Don't Say	Do Say
Pain	Situation
Challenges	Context
Problem	Scenario
Issues	Your organization

Notice the difference in tone these replacement words can have in your sales conversations:

1. Help me understand your situation...
2. Can you expand on your context...
3. You mentioned several scenarios...
4. To ensure I understand what's happening at your organization...

Notice the difference? These words are much less threatening. They're psychologically safer.

Whether you're Positioning, Exploring, or Presenting, be sure to use words that avoid tripping a negative response from your prospect. Take a look at these examples from the different movements:

Positioning: "When I talk with other CEOs, I'm hearing X, Y, and Z. Is this the ***situation*** you're experiencing, or am I off base?"

Exploring: "I appreciate the specifics you shared about your organization, is there a recent example or *scenario* you can share?"

Presenting: "Based on your *context*, you would be able to address X, Y, and Z. Does this approach seem like it would be a good fit, or is this not what you had in mind?"

What's the point with all this?

Words really do matter.

Presenting a solution well is about telling the prospect's story, envisioning their future, and allowing them to own it. It is essential for all of it to occur in a safe environment.

Chapter 12

Helping Your Prospect Get to the Finish Line

A while back, I was working on a large deal that I was really excited about. I knew it was going to have a real impact on my prospect's organization. After receiving an email giving the go ahead, I was ecstatic. I immediately put together the quote, sent it off and waited for signatures.

And waited.

And waited some more.

No response.

What happened?

The short answer is that I did not know my prospect's context well enough to get to the finish line.

When I finally did get this prospect on the phone several weeks later, she explained that before finalizing the deal, the agreement would need to receive approval from the board and the owners. It also needed to be reviewed by the CFO to secure the funds, and then go through their legal department. When I asked for her timeline for all this she told me three to six months.

I had not understood my prospect's context. Her "go ahead" meant she was ready to begin moving my solution through her organization. It did not mean the deal was closing.

As you can see, it's essential for you and your prospect to be on the same page when it comes to getting deals to the finish line. Below is a simple three-part framework to ensure nothing slips through the cracks. This framework will help you gently guide your prospect to the finish line and avoid common pitfalls.

1. Outcome timing: Get a specific date on the calendar for when your prospect would like your services in place.

Example: "When would you like to see some positive outcomes?"

What you're asking your prospect here is when they want to see the benefits of your services. Build the plan around this. Your prospect may not have thought this through yet and offer a vague answer such as, "Sometime in Q2." As the trusted guide, it is your responsibility to help your prospect flesh this out. Start by asking them to choose a specific month, and then a specific date within that month.

2. Past process: Articulate your prospect's internal process. Identify what has to happen between now and the implementation of services.

Example: "When you've hired services like ours in the past, help me understand your internal process so I can help you be successful?"

Make sure you are clear on the entire process, extending all the way to final signature. This allows you to work backwards from the date your prospect wants your services in place. You're looking to understand how things get done in your prospect's company, e.g., legal review, procurements, and/or other processes and systems. Knowing these things allows you to help them be successful in engaging your services.

3. Who: Discover who is included in the purchase decision.

Example: "To keep things moving forward for you, is there anyone else we should involve now?"

Asking this question helps you and your prospect better navigate the prospect's context. Estimates vary, but between five to ten people may have a say on a purchase decision; not just the person with whom you've been meeting. Most decisions require a number of sign offs. Understanding who those folks are will help you help your prospect navigate their internal situation.

These three parts ensure a clear plan forward to navigate the ins and outs of your prospect's environment. It allows you to build a plan to address their situation, including timing, their internal process, and any other stakeholders who could block or catapult forward the initiative.

The last step in helping your prospect to the finish line is a **written summary**, usually in the form of an email. To do this well, you will need to make sure you have taken good notes throughout the process that you can reference in your summary.

Below is an example of a written summary. I've called out each section.

Hi [first name],

Intro: It was good to talk with you, and I hope you got value from our time together. Following is a recap of what we discussed. Please let me know what I missed.

Recap the problem: The current situation is creating a number of scenarios, e.g., low performance, missed targets, and general tension among your team. This is resulting in approximately a $1 million loss in net new business, as well as lower customer satisfaction ratings.

Solution: We discussed working directly with your executive team, providing some preliminary data, and running a diagnostic to uncover the performance concerns. Your current "go live" time is April 17.

Next Steps:

1. We are targeting a follow-up meeting with your CFO, [insert name], on March 15. This meeting will last approximately 30 minutes.
2. We'll review the proposed solution and the two package options.
3. From there, the agreement goes to your legal team for final review. This review will take two to three business days.

Signature: Provided you decide to move forward, we discussed signing an agreement with your CEO, [insert name], on or before April 1.

Vision: We're looking forward to working with you to drive the mission and vision of your organization by providing you the ability to X, Y, and Z.

Confirmation: Could you please respond to this recap and confirm (or correct) this summary?

Thanks, [prospect first name],
[your name]

You can see in this short summary that the time is clear and the stakeholders are named. Their internal process is also laid out, including a date to sign the agreement. You'll notice these details are related to the problem they're looking to solve. The future state (vision) is included. There is also another ownership question, asking for confirmation of the summary.

Helping your prospect through the journey and over the finish line does not need to include the high-pressure manipulation that's so prevalent in sales. Instead, using the principles laid out in this book, selling can feel good.

***

The above sits within the three main principles of Presenting: Story, Vision, and Ownership. Did you tell your prospect's story - the story of the dragon they need to slay and how you will help them do it successfully? Did you cast a vision for the new future state of what life will be like if they work with you? Did you create a safe environment, de-risk failure, and allow your prospect to take ownership of their decision?

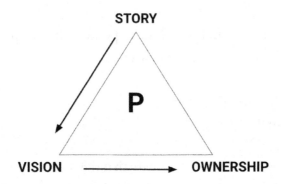

Here is the PEP system with the key selling principles.

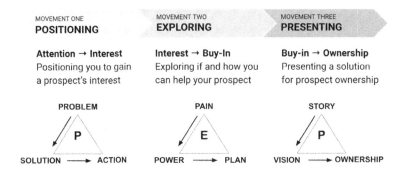

Summary of key principles with Presenting:

1. STORY - tell their story, tying your solution to their pain/problem/situation

2. VISION - cast vision of the future state of what could be if they choose to work with you

3. OWNERSHIP - create the environment that allows your prospect the freedom to own their decision

In part five ahead, you will see an example of how you can put all this together.

PART FIVE

APPLICATION
Applying Sales Principles In Your Context

Chapter 13

How You Can Put It All Together

Sales journeys have lots of twists and turns. Having a process will help you maintain the position of a trusted guide. The three movements of PEP: Attention to Interest, Interest to Buy-in, and Buy-in to Ownership provide a clear path to help your prospect find their way. By way of putting all this together, here's a real sales journey to illustrate the core principles described in this book. I've altered the scenario slightly to protect anonymity.

The largest deal I ever closed occurred in a 90-minute time span, and each of the three movements took place.

POSITIONING: Attention to Interest: I got this particular prospect's attention through a referral. The referral had mentioned to the prospect that my services may be what they were looking for. I didn't have many details, so I prepared for the call with some pre-call planning. I needed to know who it was I was talking to, a little bit about the prospect's business, and to see if I could piece together some common challenges and situations so I wasn't flying blind. The prospect showed up for the call with another executive who, I quickly discovered, was quite skeptical of my services. After the standard introductions and rapport-building, I laid out a simple agenda. As part of my agenda, I mentioned that our approach was a little different and that it wasn't for everyone so he was free to back out at any time. They said, "No, we're intrigued, keep going." That comment marked the first movement from Attention to Interest.

EXPLORING: Interest to Buy-in: From there, I jumped in with the questions I had asked permission to ask in my agenda. Within a short period of time, I discovered that this fairly new CEO was looking to solve some rather large and complex problems. He was opening new facilities, trying to staff them, and trying to stop a significant attrition rate all at the same time. Their plan for the year included aggressive expansion goals, but he could not keep his people. He admitted that he was hired to turn this around, and that the board was concerned as he was looking at a multi-million dollar attrition problem as well as a 25% shortfall on the projections to goal. At a high level, you can see that his surface level problem was stalled growth. The business impact was in the millions. His personal stake in this was high as he was feeling the pressure from the board to deliver the goods. His job was on the line. With this in mind, we identified that addressing the attrition was the top priority. I recapped what I heard and asked if he was open to exploring how we could tackle his number one concern. The response, this time from the skeptic, was, "Absolutely - anything that can get us out of this nightmare!" That remark signaled the completion of the move from Interest to Buy-in. They were ready and willing to work with me on a solution.

PRESENTING: Buy-in to Ownership: Moving into presentation mode, I told their story. "I know you're looking to grow, but you're held back by an attrition rate that, in your words, is a 'nightmare.' Unlike other solutions that typically start with candidates, we find it's better to provide you the ability to uncover business context first. In this way, you can understand what you're asking your employees to do before you even make a hire. Does this seem like it would be a helpful approach in your context, or am I off base?" He agreed. I proceeded in this way throughout the presentation, pausing to ask ownership questions. Toward the end, I asked, "I've shown you a lot, but what have I missed? Is there something you were hoping to see that I haven't covered in order to address your turnover?" They both replied, "Nope - this is great - love it. I can see us using this right away." I asked, "When would you like to see this go live in your organization?" We settled on the first of the following month. I asked my prospect to help me understand what their internal process was when they purchased something like my services. He replied, "I need to run it by my legal team, but that's it." I asked if there was anyone else that we should bring in now to avoid any delays later on. He said no. Then I asked, "What else do you need from me in order to make a decision?" The CEO replied,

"How much?" I gave him a quote, and he agreed to the price. I sent a written summary of our conversation along with the agreement. The agreement was signed the following morning.

Certainly, not all sales conversations go this way. Buyers do not always follow your process, no matter how good it is. They may buyin, but then lose interest. Or, you may get all the way to ownership, but something else takes priority. There is no perfect system. However, the core principles outlined in this book and these three movements work because they are based on how humans work. They help your prospects to become the hero in a way that feels good to both you and your new client.

Fun fact: my sales manager at the time listened to the call that I outlined above. He made fifty-one bullet-point comments of things that I did wrong. Fifty-one! I had interrupted my prospect. I talked too much at times. I got off track, and I missed other important questions. He was right. I thanked him and I continued to improve. You, too, will make mistakes. Don't worry; you don't have to get everything perfectly right in order to help someone. The key is remembering that *helping* is the goal, not delivering a perfect sales pitch. When you make this shift, you will find you can feel good about selling.

Chapter 14

Handling The Three Most Common Objections

Objection-handling is a big topic in sales. Opinions are loud and they vary widely. Because of this, it's important to back up and ask, what is an objection? Merriam-Webster has three definitions, two of which relate to sales. They are:

1. a reason or argument presented in opposition
2. a feeling or expression of disapproval

Most salespeople respond to the first definition. They stick to reasons and logic. This is a mistake. All you end up doing is arguing with your hero. In reality, definition number two is far more important. Every objection is an emotional response. It's a feeling. Even the ones shrouded in reason. Because of this, responding to the emotion is more effective.

But what causes sales objections?

Fair warning: you may hate my primary answer about the main cause of sales objections.

Ready?

It's your fault.

That's right. Many objections from your prospects are your fault. They are the result of you doing something wrong. Whether it's annoying tactics, failing to listen, the words you use, or not setting appropriate expectations, somewhere along the line, you created the objections. Sales professionals spend a lot of time training people to handle objections. They spend very little time on helping you to avoid them. This creates a vicious cycle in which you are learning to handle the objections you created in the first place. That doesn't feel good!

Here's the good news: if you practice the sales principles in this book, you will avoid creating many objections in the first place. To be clear, you will still get objections. But they won't be the ones you could have avoided from the get-go.

While there are any number of objections, the three most common are **price**, **status quo**, and **time/bandwidth**. Let's take each in turn.

Objection #1: Price

The first is the classic price objection. No matter the price, your prospect, having been conditioned by advertising and manipulative sales techniques, may object to your pricing. Your prospect may stall, pause, or outright complain that the price is too high. Most salespeople respond either by justifying their pricing or reducing it. Both tactics are bad and do not address the emotions at play. By justifying their pricing, they are, in essence, arguing with their prospect instead of making them the hero. By lowering the price, they reduce the value of their product or service and hurt their reputation as a trusted guide. Below, I've outlined ten ways to respond to the emotions behind price objections that are more effective than justification or price reduction.

1. Acknowledge: Acknowledge the prospect's position and offer an out. This might sound something like this: "I'm sorry you feel that the price is too high. Should we end the conversation here?" A common response from prospects is, "No, no, it's fine."

2. Ask for clarity: Request that your prospect help you understand where they're coming from. For example: "Could you tell me more?" Or, "What makes you say that?" This shows that you're open to listening, and it places the objection-handling into the hands of the prospect. It's their objection. You just need to help them navigate it.

3. Pause: Rather than respond immediately to a price objection, allow for a moment of quiet. Just pause. This provides time for your prospect to think through the pricing and their initial response. I once had a prospect say, "Wow, that much! Hmm...I wasn't expecting that." I paused, saying nothing as he mulled it over in his head. Then he stopped and said, "Well, now that I think about it, it's going to save me more than it costs, so I'm actually ahead of the game. Let's do it!" That's the power of the pause.

4. Repeat: Repeat back what your prospect says to help them think it through. I had a prospect say, "Man, that's way more than I expected." Rather than the typical sales response of, "What were you expecting?" (which risks tripping psychological reactance), I repeated back the last few words, saying, "It's more than you expected…" and then I waited. His next sentence was, "But I think I can manage it." Psychologists repeat back words to help their patients work through a problem. As a trusted guide, you can do the same.

5. Reflect: Price objections from your prospect can be quite intense and emotional. You can reflect back with professionalism. In one instance, my prospect had a strong knee-jerk reaction, saying, "Whoa - that much! My God, really!" I said, "Whoa - that sounds like that's a deal breaker! Am I reading you right?" He immediately settled down and said, "No, not really, I guess I just didn't know." Not knowing creates feelings of fear and anxiety - fear of the unknown; hence, you can get intense reactions.

6. Invite Input: Invite prospects to solve their own objection. Sometimes a simple invitation is all that is needed. I had a prospect tell me, "I don't think I can get the money for this." I said, "It sounds like we're at an impasse. What should we do about that?" He thought about it for a few seconds and then said, "Actually, I'm good. I can draw the funds from another budget."

7. Reframe: Help your prospect focus on the gain rather than the expense - but do it without manipulation. I once heard one of my sales reps say, "Sure, I appreciate the price concern. Although, to put it in perspective, you likely spend more on pizza for your employees than you would to solve what we've been talking about. Is that a fair statement, or am I off base?" It was a powerful reframe. The deal closed that day. As stated earlier, reframes are not meant to be used in a manipulative way, but to help your prospect see clearly. Oftentimes your prospect can get so focused on an *expense* that they forget the *gain*.

8. Provide Perspective/Big Picture: Help your prospect to see the broader picture of what's at stake. In some cases, you may need to be a little more direct in order to help your prospect. That is, you may need to provide a stark contrast. One response you can use is, "I appreciate your budgetary concerns; however, based on our conversation, you're already spending the money. In fact, if we can get you even halfway to where you need to be, you'll be net positive. Working with us won't cost you anything. Is that a fair statement, or did I step out of bounds?" You can also help them to visualize the bigger picture. Begin with a question like, "Is cost the only factor in your purchase decision, or are there other considerations." This helps to refocus the conversation on value to the organization. Skip Miller, author of *ProActive Selling*, notes that there are five areas that executives are concerned with: ROI, Brand,

Leverage, Risk, and Time. These are all areas worth exploring to help your prospect see the bigger picture of what's at stake.

9. Collaborate: Ensure the price objection is really about price. Sometimes, prospects are fine with your price, they just have to find a way within their organization to make it happen. Asking, "Is it a matter of finding the money or something else?" can open the conversation, allowing you to help your prospect to think it through. There are CEO slush funds, training budgets, and other discretionary funds that can be tapped if your prospect sees you as the solution.

10. Add Value: Rather than reducing or justifying the price, consider adding value. This may be in the form of an added service or additional resources. I was working with one of my sales representatives who was trying to get a deal done by month's end. They had settled on a mutually agreeable price; however, the prospect wanted his managers to be included in one of the training sessions. Unfortunately, the package and price point didn't leave any room for that. What to do?

1. Option one - hold the line and risk the deal
2. Option two - allow more people into the training at the same rate and devalue the service
3. Option 3 - provide added value

We opted for option three and provided additional value with a "mini training." That is, rather than an official, by the book training, my sales representative agreed to run a 90-minute virtual training for the additional managers. It was a creative response. The prospect was happy. The deal was closed that day.

It can be tempting to start dropping your price at the first hint of an objection. It can also be easy to get defensive and justify your price. Resist these temptations. Instead, get clear on the objection by responding to the emotion. There is certainly a time and place to work out a deal. More often, though, the ten suggestions above will help you help your prospect solve their price objection.

Objection #2: Status Quo

Another prevalent objection salespeople encounter is status quo. That is, your prospect is content to do nothing. They're satisfied with the way things are. In terms of a feeling - they're content. Why? Simple. Things aren't bad enough to change. This can be a hard one to crack, but we'll look at some ways to help them. Following are four ways to help them get unstuck:

1. Exploring - The goal of exploring in the PEP selling system is to help your prospect move from general Interest to Buy-in (i.e., a willingness to do something different). Getting under the surface and exploring business impact from multiple angles helps your prospect quantify their situation in such a way as to recognize they need to change something, e.g., work with you. When this isn't done well, prospects will not see enough reason to change. Thus, it's critical to find out what really matters to your prospect with thorough exploration - whether classic or rapid discovery.

2. Stakes - Sometimes in order to help someone make a positive change, you need to help them see what's at stake - both positive and negative stakes. In sales there is a tendency to talk about the positive features and benefits of a product or service - and this can certainly be helpful. But unpacking the negative stakes is critical too. Pain (or negative stakes) is considered the stronger motivator thanks to psychologist Daniel Khanneman's loss aversion theory. However, this beloved theory has been debunked, according to Professor David Gal from the University of Illinois. Theory aside, what's important is helping your prospect by seeing both the positives and negatives at play for them. The best salespeople have known this for ages, but I'm grateful to Don Miller's "stakes" language. For example, when a prospect states that they are losing good employees, asking how that is impacting morale, current managers, social reputation, and the bottom line can help them understand more fully the negative stakes. At the same time, the positive stakes of the solution could be an improved culture, morale, lower attrition, better brand and reputation, and higher profit margins.

3. De-risk - De-risk change. Picture a child at the edge of a pool anxious to jump into their parent's arms. They're scared to leave the safety of solid ground and jump into the unknown. To de-risk means to help your prospect take the leap - to help them know they'll be successful. Like the child afraid to jump into the pool, make it clear that your prospect will successfully land in mom or dad's arms. Your prospect's reputation or job may be on the line. De-risking the path to success can break the status quo. In their upcoming book, *The Jolt Effect*, authors

Matthew Dixon and Ted McKenna note that risk is the greatest deterrent to a prospect moving forward. I'm thankful to Aaron Evans' video about this as the book won't be available until late 2022. Internet marketers, too, have known about de-risking for decades. It's why you see money back guarantees on a lot of digital products right near the "Buy Now" button. They're removing the risk. In your sales conversations, presentations, and proposals, removing risk is done through PEP. Positioning yourself to stand out as someone who can solve their problem. Creating a safe environment to Explore what matters most. Presenting a clear path and providing free-choice reduces risk. Anything you can do to de-risk things for your prospect, the better. Your context will dictate what levers you can pull. Consider the following: support systems, white glove treatment, testimonials, free trials, case studies, and training. Simple steps and a clear path help to de-risk change.

4. Tell a story - We're wired for stories, so use them in your sales conversations. Storyteller Jyoti Guptara notes that a "good story beats great information." Story guru Kindra Hall suggests a three-part framework that can be quite powerful in helping people break status quo. It is simply: Normal > Explosion > New Normal. Essentially, your prospect is living what they perceive to be the norm. If you can tell a story of how things have changed (explosion) and that a new normal is required for their context and their success, your prospect will be much more likely to hear you and be willing to change. For example, think of how retail sales had to change to a new normal in light of the explosion of the Internet. Think of how businesses have had to adapt to the pandemic. The old way is gone. There's a new reality, requiring new methods and approaches. No one wants to get left behind. Help them see the new reality with a story.

5. Reframe - Helping prospects reframe the situation can be effective in breaking the status quo. I once had a prospect who dug their heels in, saying, "We never sign agreements without an out clause." That was their status quo. It was how they did business. Their request was perfectly fine if they were buying a washing machine - that's why there are warranties. I wasn't selling an appliance, though. My response was, "I appreciate that, but your request puts me in the position of an unequal partner in your success. This wouldn't be good for either of us. Should we just part ways now?" In other words, instead of arguing over legalese, I reframed the situation in the light of our mutually beneficial relationship. This broke through their status quo and the deal closed a week later. Status quo thinking can show up in any number of ways. The reframe helps your prospect see things in a new light. While you should never be smug about it, the fact is that doing things the same way got them to where they are. Helping them see things anew is a good thing.

A fantastic approach to challenging the status quo objection is Geico's famous ad about car insurance. You may know it:

"15 minutes could save you 15% or more on car insurance."

How does this challenge the status quo? Isn't this just about being cheaper? No. The point here is that getting someone to change their insurance (their status quo) is hard. Consider what 15% would save you. Let's say your car insurance costs $100 per month. Would you go through all the hassle to switch for the *chance* to save $15 per month ($180 per year)? It's a lot of work for such a low return - and it's not guaranteed (hence the word "could" in the slogan). However, Geico is not done. They've also made it super easy - 15 minutes. If it's only an investment of 15 minutes, now it may be worth a look. It's a brilliant strategy to address the real objection to switching car insurance - status quo.

Objection #3 - Time/Bandwidth

The third most common objection is time/bandwidth. Time is the most valuable commodity of all, and time constraints are a reality. Your prospects are busy. Things are often in flux, and folks do not have the time or bandwidth to address certain situations in light of other priorities. The good news is there are a number of ways to navigate time/bandwidth objections.

To be clear, you do want to honor your prospect's timeline. Pressure tactics to close the deal earlier (or on your timeline) can be off-putting. An assured new client is better than a fast deal that falls apart. There are cases where you can achieve both. Here are five approaches you can take:

1. Quantify the wait. Prospects may not recognize that waiting to solve their particular situation may make things worse. For example, if you have a client who is losing $1,000,000 annually, waiting until next quarter will cost them $250,000 in the meantime. They may be okay with that, but it's perfectly acceptable to call it out. A gentle, "I'm happy to get started next quarter; I just want to ensure you're okay with the cost of delay in the interim. It's totally up to you, but should we explore options to roll this out sooner?"

2. Quick wins. Similar to adding value with price objections, if there are quick wins you can provide, this can overcome the time/bandwidth objection. It doesn't have to be revenue, either. For example, I once had a prospect who wanted to wait to address a tricky situation with employee engagement. When I showed how they could get a quick win with some key managers, the value of my services increased. We closed the deal that day instead of the following month. In short, you can use the idea of quick wins to see if it resonates with your prospect.

3. Help with bandwidth. There are a number of ways that you can assist your prospect with overcoming time or bandwidth challenges. The first is by putting together a timeline that works with your prospect's schedule. Timelines allow your prospect to see that not everything has to be done at once. Remember there are emotions behind objections. With the time/bandwidth objection, it's the feeling of being overwhelmed. You can review the order of events your prospect has on their plate to show how they can maintain their current duties, without adding additional work. For example, in one case, my prospect wanted to wait until they made a key hire to take over the responsibility of working with me. Why? They were overwhelmed and didn't have the bandwidth. Rather than wait, I suggested we work together to identify that key hire to make sure they were getting the right person for the job. She agreed. Instead of waiting for what could have been months, we implemented my services and my client got value right away to do something she was going to have to spend time doing anyway. In other words, I used my service to help address her feelings of being overwhelmed. You can't always do this, but when you can, you will differentiate yourself from all the other folks trying to push things on busy prospects.

4. Incentivize with care. You can use incentives to buy time. One of my dad's favorite expressions is, "Money talks." Leveraging price can indeed get deals over the line faster. People like to feel like they got a deal. However, most sales people lead with this one, dropping the price for a quick close. While this can be effective, it needs to be used with care. You don't want to minimize the value of your services, and you don't want to pressure your prospect. To do this well, here are three principles to keep in mind.

1. Find out what will motivate your buyer. It's often not money. Always ask, e.g., "Are there any things we could do to help us get started sooner, or should we stick to the original timeline?"

2. Know that state of the deal. A deal that has gone quiet is very different from a deal that's right on the line. They require different approaches.

3. Don't be a jerk. This should be common sense, but the amount of pressure tactics I see suggest a reminder on this is in order. Help, don't pressure.

5. Timing matters. From his research, Dan Pink notes that, "Timing is not everything. Everything is timing." His point in regard to sales is that ends matter. People like to wrap things up. There is a feeling of accomplishment. There is a natural desire for completion. So in terms of selling, help your hero do that. Leveraging the end of the week, month, quarter, and year are all ways to help your prospects bring closure to their world by signing an agreement and working with you.

***

To recap, objections are often the result of poor sales techniques and processes. That is, you trigger negative emotions that create objections. That said, the big three will come up for you no matter how well you do. Importantly, it's not your job to overcome objections. It's your job to guide your prospect so that they can overcome their objection.

To make sure you address the emotions and feelings at play, you want to validate, empathize, and teach. The following framework will help. It's called VET. This stands for: Validate, Empathize, Teach. The VET framework allows you to adapt the responses above to a variety of objections & situations.

/vet/ (verb) - the acronym VET has the added bonus of lining up with the definition of the word vet, or vetting, e.g., make a careful and critical examination of something. When selling, you want to help your prospect VET their objection.

Validate: Validating someone can take many forms, but in a sales context, it might sound like: "I appreciate that you brought that up. It's a fair point." This simple statement "validates" the feeling. This makes people feel good. It also shows that you are someone who is emotionally aware. People will feel safe with you.

Empathize: Empathizing with a prospect in a sales scenario might sound like this: "It sounds like you weren't expecting that." Or, "I can see why that might be frustrating." These short empathic statements acknowledge the emotions at play. It puts people at ease. It makes you trustworthy.

Teach: Teaching might sound like this: "Are you open to thinking about this a bit differently, or should we end our conversation here?" This provides safety and freedom of choice for your prospect to **Talk** and/or **Think** it through. Or, the objection may indeed be a deal breaker, in which case **Termination** is the best course of action. You are then free to move on to helping someone who needs your services.

When you put it altogether, it sounds like something like this:

"I appreciate that you brought that up. It's a fair point. It sounds like you weren't expecting that, am I reading you right?"

Yes - I didn't know...

"Totally get it, are you open to thinking about this a bit differently, or should we end our conversation here?"

***

The VET objection framework and the suggestions above will help you find your way in most sales situations. As always, tone matters along with a spirit of helping your hero along their journey.

In the following chapter, you will see how you can prepare for objections in advance. You will learn a simple approach to get a better understanding of your prospect's situation to help you better help them.

Chapter 15

Pre-call Planning That Will Help You Help Your Prospect

Why did I save pre-call planning for the end? Context. Without seeing sales in a new light, pre-call planning becomes an exercise in getting an upper hand rather than offering a helping hand. I've seen too many salespeople take their newly gleaned insights and knowledge and try to sweep in and save the day. Because their head is so full of information, they make assumptions rather than ask. This is not the purpose of pre-call planning. Here are three reason why it's so important to your sales efforts:

1. Mindset: Pre-call planning helps to get you into the right mindset to craft tailored messaging, offer deep insights, and to show prospects you are a trusted guide. The right mindset is a helping mindset, e.g., how can I help this prospect with their problem? Even cursory research provides wonderful information to help you hone in on what may matter to your prospect. You will be able to more effectively navigate their world. Not to mention that every prospect appreciates that you cared enough to do some homework!

2. Scope: Pre-call planning can help you scope the size of your opportunity. The amount of information you are able to collect/not collect will give you a good indicator as to the level of effort (scope) you should put into working each lead. For example, if you realize this is a brand new venture, there may be limited resources and information available. Clearly there will be only so much you can do. On the other hand, established organizations may have an overwhelming amount of information, requiring you to scope your research to specific areas that matter to your prospect.

3. Possibilities: Pre-call planning allows you to imagine possibilities to help your prospect and anticipate potential objections. You can begin to piece together their story and the dragons they may need to slay in their particular niche or industry. I was once working with a logistics company. In my research, I discovered that they were undergoing a massive digital transformation as an industry. It was creating a lot of headaches. Sure enough, my prospect brought it up during our conversation. Because I had reflected on how I might be able to help in this area, I showed her how my services directly impacted her digital transformation initiatives. The deal closed and even expanded to additional parts of the organization.

With this brief backdrop, here are three simple things you can do to ensure you're well-equipped to help your prospect.

Learn about the individual

1. The first is the most obvious - learn more about who the person is you'll be helping. Find out what their role/title is, how long they have been there, who they report to, where they went to school, where they live, whether they have a blog or write articles for their organization…etc.

Learn about the company

2. The second is to take some time to learn more about their company and what it is they do. Start with their why. What's their mission? Why do they do what they do? What's their industry, niche, speciality? Who are their competitors? What's happening with this industry due to the economy, time of year, etc.? One way to think about this is to know so much about the company that you could work there. If organizations start offering you a job after their conversations with you, you're on the right track.

Learn about their story

3. The third thing is to put yourself in your prospect's shoes. Seek to understand what some of the stories may be based on your research. Are they growing? If so, how might this growth be impacting them? Has there been a reorganization, or new CEO, and, if so, how might this impact things for them? Are

there current events, webinars, LinkedIn posts, or Google News that can shed some light on what's happening in their world?

A simple checklist like the one below can help you streamline your pre-call planning:

About the individual(s)

- ☐ Title/role
- ☐ Location
- ☐ Length at current company
- ☐ Anything newsworthy (blogs, press mentions)
- ☐ Explore LinkedIn profile (career track, experience)
- ☐ Explore company website (review team page)

About the company

- ☐ What do they do (industry)
- ☐ Org website (about us page, their mission, careers page)
- ☐ What do they care about
- ☐ Press mentions
- ☐ Glassdoor page
- ☐ Company LinkedIn page
- ☐ Estimated headcount

What's their story?

- ☐ Reflect on what you think they are going through. What progress do you think they need to make, and how might you be able to help with your services?

- ☐ Typically, companies are in one of five phases: Startup, Growth, Maturing, Decline, or Revival. Knowing where a company is can help you understand their situation more clearly:

1. **Startup**: New, fast-moving, lots of change and chaos - exciting times
2. **Growing**: Booming, moving fast, and concerned about all the change and impact on culture
3. **Maturing**: Things are slowing down, less frantic, trying to avoid shrinking profit margins
4. **Decline**: Low sales, short on cash, losing to competitors
5. **Revival**: Trying to reinvent themselves, new products/services, new approach

This checklist is available as a download in the appendix. Remember, a little homework goes a long way to helping your heroes reach their goals.

The final chapter in this book will summarize the steps and principles you can take to feel good about selling. Using the principles in this book will simultaneously put you in the trusted guide position and help you to avoid the things that can be so off-putting in sales.

Chapter 16

Principles That Will Boost Your Confidence and Help Your Sales

To be clear, this book doesn't contain everything you need to know about sales - no one book can. Rather, my hope is that it will help you avoid the things that bother you (and your prospects) about sales, and to help you feel good about selling. Hopefully, you have begun to see sales in a new light. People need help. Sales is about helping people. Helping people is a good thing. This feels good. You can do it in three simple movements:

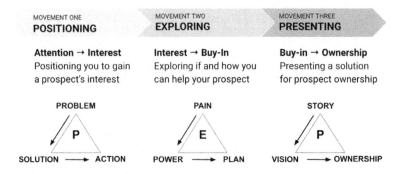

PEP empowers you to help your prospects find their way in the dark. Below is a recap of what we explored.

POSITIONING: Attention to Interest: In order to get someone's interest, you need to be seen - you need to stand out. Being clear on the problem you solve for your prospects is vital. Speaking human and hitting the primal brain with contrast is a really great way of doing this. You can also stand out as something different. A well-placed reframe will help you capture your prospect's interest. Unlike other sales books that force a system on you, imagine being taught just a few principles that empower you to sell effectively and with dignity. Is that something worth exploring, or is that not what you had in mind? See what I did there? That was contrast, wrapped up in reframe, ending with an ownership question. The three principles at play are:

1. PROBLEM
2. SOLUTION
3. ACTION

EXPLORING: Interest to Buy-in: To take someone's interest and help them buy in to working with you, you need to understand what matters to them. Whether through classic or rapid discovery, you need to ask great questions, listen well, and explore the problem that needs solving (pain). To do this well, you need to create a safe environment. You also need to be talking with the person(s) who can actually do something about it, and make a plan with them. The three principles at play are:

1. PAIN
2. POWER
3. PLAN

PRESENTING: Buy-in to Ownership: you'll notice this is a sales path that is steeped in your prospect's story - their journey. You are the trusted guide helping your hero slay their dragons. Understanding your prospect's story beyond typical surface-level pain allows you to cast a vision for a new future. This is a journey that begins and ends with your prospect taking ownership. It's up to them to take your help - or not. This is their story, their pain, their risk, their journey, and their future. You are not the hero. You are there to show what's possible for your prospect with your solution. All the while, you are creating a space so they can make the decision for themselves. The three principles at play are:

1. STORY
2. VISION
3. OWNERSHIP

Positioning, Exploring, and Presenting (PEP) provide a clear and simple path to help you guide your prospects. Keep the focus on the problem you solve for your customer. Invite them to take a journey with you, and allow them to step into a new future supported by your services.

***

Sales has changed - drastically. Buyers are no longer willing to tolerate traditional sales tactics and manipulation. The future will bring more change. There will be more automation, more technology, and more try-before-you-buy. The salesperson who is the trusted guide will maintain a critical role helping prospects find their way to navigate the noise and confusion.

Take a second to re-read the definition of sales in this book, below.

"Sales is the process of helping someone make a positive change and allowing them to own it."

Imagine what would happen to your sales and to your customer's experience if you go and do that.

To your success!

Sincerely,
~Ted Olson
PS - take your sales to the next level with the PEP Certification Course, below.

Taking Your Sales To The Next Level

This book has been written to create awareness of a better sales approach, and to provide you a fresh path forward. I hope it has done that. If you want to gain mastery level, I encourage you to get certified in the PEP Selling System through the **PEP Certification Course**.

Go to: FeelGoodAboutSelling.com

This on-demand course will allow you to hear and practice the principles discussed in this book so you can gain mastery.

You'll get:

- Easy-to-absorb videos & materials
- Sales playbooks & worksheets
- Checkpoints to measure your progress
- A Certificate acknowledging your PEP Certification

Go to FeelGoodAboutSelling.com and subscribe. If you're already a subscriber - great - you'll be notified when the course is ready. This course will help you (or your sales team) thrive and sell in ways that feel good to everyone. Join the movement to non-salesy selling!

Subscribe today at: FeelGoodAboutSelling.com

About Ted Olson

Ted Olson has helped thousands of sales professionals feel good about their sales and marketing efforts. He is the founder of **Feel Good About Selling**, the book and sales training program designed for people who want to increase their sales and keep their integrity. Ted has been in sales longer than he cares to admit, and throughout that time he has helped sales teams and individuals break records. When not training salespeople, Ted practices martial arts and homeschools his four kids with his wife, Nicole. They have two dogs (Oatmeal and Honeybee) and a guinea pig (Pinball). His kids wanted him to add this last part about the pets.

Visit FeelGoodAboutSelling.com to learn more.

Appendix

Downloadable Sales Guides

Visit the resources page at FeelGoodAboutSelling.com to download any of these eight sales guides:

1. The Pre-Call Planning Checklist
2. Positioning You Well (PSA)
3. Creating a Safe Environment (Agenda Guide)
4. Asking Great Questions Checklist
5. Demo/Presentation Checklist
6. Objection Handling Guide
7. Email Follow Up Template
8. Getting Deals Unstuck Guide

Here's the resource page link:
https://feelgoodaboutselling.com/resources/

References

Notes, Nods, and Citations

Notes & Nods

I've done my best to reference and cite the ideas in this book. The challenge is that sales ideas are often recycled and modified making it hard to know where they came from. Hence I created this notes and nods section to call out some of the origins where I could. Direct quotes and/or ideas are under the citations section.

The Title

I was struggling with a title for this book for months. I went through several iterations, but nothing felt right. One day I was listening to Dr. J.J. Peterson from Don Miller's organization, Business Made Simple. In their podcast, Peterson was describing how he helped his niece market her flowers at a yard sale. He asked her a question along the lines of, "How do you want people to feel when they buy the flowers that you're selling in these jars?" She said, "Joy!" Peterson said, so you're selling "Joy in a Jar."

I asked myself a similar question.

How do I want people to feel after they read this book or engage with my sales training?

I want people to "Feel Good About Selling." And that's how I came up with the title that landed, stuck, and felt good.

Part One: Rethinking Sales

Chapter 1: Reasons You May Not Feel Good About Selling

The list of books in this chapter were chosen at random through an Amazon search. I have great respect for people in sales and the sales leaders who have written books to help people sell more effectively. However, the titles of the books reflect a male-dominated nomenclature. The aggression reflected in these titles is uncomfortable - and unnecessary. It no longer resonates with today's buyers and many sellers.

Chapter 2: A Different Way to Think About Sales

The definition of sales outlined in this book was adapted from one of my sales mentors who adapted it from someone else, who adapted it from someone else, who adapted...okay, you get the idea.

Chapter 3: Your Unique Role in the Sales Journey

The Zig Zigler quote in this chapter is quoted often in sales. I pulled it from an Entrepreneur.com article (see citation).

Although the hero's journey is not new, I lean on some of Donald Miller's work. Check out *The Building of a Story*

Brand (see citation). Also, check out his site, BusinessMadeSimple.com - good stuff there, too.

Chapter 4: A Different Kind of Sales Approach

The reference to the character Arnold Horseshack comes from a show I grew up watching as a kid. The show was called, *Welcome Back, Kotter*. I linked a Youtube video under citations to show a scene that reflects how many try to be heard and seen in their marketing efforts. You may get a good laugh.

I referenced a famous Bruce Lee quote and linked a YouTube clip under citations. As a practitioner of Wing Chun, I became a Bruce Lee fan. His philosophy on martial arts can be summed up in the remark "Be like water." I feel the same way about sales. If you try to force a sales methodology rather than adapting and being flexible, it's much harder. It doesn't feel good. PEP was designed to "be like water."

Part Two: Positioning You To Stand Out

Chapter 5: Your Public Service Announcement

I have to give a nod to infomercials regarding the PSA. They're just so good at highlighting the problem, showing the solution, and calling you to action. I also studied Internet Marketing in the early 2000's and have been tinkering with writing sales copy ever since. Among other things, I learned to highlight the problem, stir it up, and then offer a solution. I also want to give a nod to Donald Miller as he does a great job unpacking the ancient art of storytelling with his story framework (see citation).

Chapter 6: The Power of Contrast

I cite the book, *Persuasion Code*. I met one of the authors at a talk where he outlined the research. The points on speaking to the primal brain are profound (see citation).

Regarding Maya Angelou - I've heard this quote for decades. Some argue she may not have said it first, but the point is still valid (see citation).

Mac vs. PC ads (see citation). These ads are hilarious and provide great lessons and insights in marketing.

Chapter 7: The Power of Reframe

Challenger sales books - If you're going to read these, read them both. I'd suggest *Challenger Sale* first, then *Challenger Customer*.

Reagan-Mondale debate - If you want to see the ultimate reframe, this is it (see citation).

Mandela quote - I can't remember where I first heard this. It may have been a movie or documentary, but I did see it in an article by INC.com (see citation).

Chapter 8: Helping You Stand Out

I want to give a nod to Nancy Martini. Nancy is an amazing salesperson. The early development of the PSA can be traced back to what she called a "result sentence." That is, don't tell people what you do, tell them what you do for them. Her book, *Customer-Focused Selling*, while now dated, is filled with common-sense and practical advice for anyone in sales. She was a pioneer in putting the customer first when it came to selling.

Movie trailer idea - The positioning statement as a movie trailer idea comes from my friend and colleague, Kevin Rhedin. His thought was instrumental in helping me to realize the whole sequence of PEP as a movie.

The Like Switch - A really great book on human behavior. Highly recommend it (see citation).

Gong - Gong's tool and data are super helpful in creating high-performing sales teams. When I first started using Gong I was stunned at how low my patience score was. I thought I was better than that. I wasn't. Data matters.

Part Three: Exploring Need In A Safe Environment

Chapter 9: How To Have Great Sales Conversations

Selling systems - There are so many great sales methodologies. I've been exposed to bits and pieces of many of them, and have used several extensively. They include, but are not limited to: The Sandler Selling System, MEDDIC, Miller-Heimann, Challenger, SPIN, and Consultative Selling.

Leadership Triangle - A mentor of mine recommended this book. It's a powerful message on the three key facets of leadership. Sales draws a lot from leadership principles. Selling is leadership (see citation).

Conscious Selling - A mentor introduced the three levels of pain to me. Based on some research, I believe they come from Ganesh. I'm less familiar with this sales methodology, but getting under the surface is vital in helping people, and a must-do practice to effectively help people.

Brehm's work - When I was first introduced to psychological reactance by a sales mentor, I was shocked at how often I was tripping reactance in others. I was unintentionally making sales harder. Once you see it in yourself, you can easily overcome this.

The framework for asking great questions comes from psychology. Imagine sitting down with a therapist and opening up about your struggles. The first question/statement they'll often start with is "Tell me more." A full list of 12 questions in this light was introduced to me by one of my sales mentors. However, I shortened it to 6 questions to make it easier to follow and more efficient and adaptable to various contexts.

Adam Grant - This was a timely quote I stumbled upon on LinkedIn. It was during the time I was writing about the core sales principle of freedom of choice.

Chapter 10: Creating A Safe Environment

Tommy Boy - This movie is a classic - a must watch!

Psychological safety - Google's research on what makes a great team is excellent.

Part Four: Presenting For Ownership

Chapter 11: How to Present a Solution So That Your Prospect Owns It

Trigger words - Another sales mentor introduced me to certain words that risk tripping psychological reactance.

Chapter 12: Helping Your Prospect Get to the Finish Line

Get it in writing - I remember bemoaning this step in the sales process as overkill. While it won't necessarily make or break a deal, it helps to keep everyone aligned and clear. That's never a bad thing.

Part Five: Applying Sales Principles In Your Context

Chapter 13: How You can Put It All Together

Gartner - The 2018 Gartner Sales & Marketing Conference in Las Vegas confirmed my own experience and research and highlighted several areas that have helped me to grow in my sales knowledge and to help others feel good about selling.

Chapter 14: Handling the Three Most Common Objections

Chris Voss - His book, *Never Split The Difference* is loved by sales people. Chris has a number of YouTube videos worth watching, too. I've learned from him and am indebted to his work. I do find (in some instances) those who lean into his work slant toward manipulation and tactics, which doesn't feel good (see citation).

Skip Miller - *Proactive Selling* - great book, worth the read (see citation). My big takeaway was the 5 different value points that executives care about. It helps people see things from more than one angle.

Dan Pink - I saw Dan Pink speak at the 2018 Gartner Sales & Marketing Conference in Las Vegas. He was citing fascinating research from his book *When: The Scientific Secrets of Perfect Timing* (see citation).

Chapter 15: Pre-call Planning That Helps You Help Your Prospect

Growth phase - There are a decent amount of articles and research on growth phases. It is not my area of expertise, but these phases can help sales people more effectively understand the needs of an organization at any given time. I listed two articles in the citations section of the book.

Chapter 16: Principles That Will Help You Feel Good About Selling

Speaking human - This idea was drawn from the book *Persuasion Code* (see citation).

Checklists - you'll notice that many of the downloadable sales guides are checklists. Checklists have helped me to create one-page sales playbooks that everyone can agree to and follow. For a great book on the power of checklists, check out *The Checklist Manifesto* (see citation).

Citations

Adamson, B., Dixon, M., Spenner, P., & Toman, N. (2015). *The Challenger Customer: Selling to the Hidden Influencer Who Can Multiply Your Results.* Penguin.

Angelou, M. (2017, November 13). *Let's save Maya Angelou from fake quotes.* BBC.com. https://www.bbc.com/news/41913640

Apple. (2009, October 28). *Mac Vs PC commercials - Cancel or Allow?* YouTube.com. https://www.youtube.com/watch?v=8CwoluNRSSc

Belfort, J. (2017). *Way of the Wolf: Straight Line Selling: Master the Art of Persuasion, Influence, and Success.* Gallery Books.

Blount, J. (2015). *Fanatical Prospecting: The Ultimate Guide for Starting Sales Conversations and Filling the Pipeline by Leveraging Social Selling, Telephone, E-Mail, and Cold Calling.* John Wiley & Sons.

Brehm, J. (n.d.). *Brehm's Reactance Theory: Definition & Overview*. Study.com. https://study.com/academy/lesson/brehms-reactance-theory-definition-lesson-quiz.html#:~:text=In%201966%2C%20psychologist%20Jack%20Brehm,when%20freedom%20is%20being%20threatened.&text=Brehm's%20Reactance%20Theory%20also%20states,larger%20the%20resistance%20

Campbell, J. (1990). *The Hero's Journey: Joseph Campbell on His Life and Work (The Collected Works of Joseph Campbell)*. Harper & Row.

Cardone, G. (2018). *Sell or Be Sold: How to Get Your Way in Business and in Life*. FlashReads.

Carnegie, D. (1936). *How to Win Friends & Influence People*. Pocket Books.

CFI. (n.d.). *Corporate Finance Institute*. https://corporatefinanceinstitute.com/.

https://corporatefinanceinstitute.com/resources/knowledge/finance/business-life-cycle/#:~:text=The%20business%20life%20cycle%20is,dollars%20or%20various%20financial%20metrics.

Dixon, M., & Adamson, B. (2013). *The Challenger Sale: Taking Control of the Customer Conversation*. Penguin.

Dixon, M., & McKenna, T. (2022). *The Jolt Effect: How High Performers Overcome Customer Indecision*. Portfolio. https://www.linkedin.com/posts/aaronevanssalesenablement_sales-salestips-activity-6913019608614526976-JlYX?utm_source=linkedin_share&utm_medium=member_desktop_web

Duarte, N. (2010). *Resonate: Present Visual Stories That Transform Audiences* (1st ed.). John Wiley and Sons. https://www.duarte.com/resonate-book/

Eagleman, D. (2021). *Livewired: The Inside Story of the Ever-Changing Brain*. Vintage.

Eha, B. P. (2012, November 12). *Zig Ziglar and the Importance of Helping Others*. Entrepreneur. Retrieved July 15, 2021, from

https://www.entrepreneur.com/article/225131

Foley, J. (Director). (1992). *Glengarry Glen Ross* [Film]. New Line Cinema.

Ford, K., & Tucker, K. (2013). *The Leadership Triangle: The Three Options That Will Make You a Stronger Leader* (Kindle ed.). Morgan James Publishing.

Gal, D. (2018, July 31). Why the Most Important Idea in Behavioral Decision-Making Is a Fallacy. *Scientific American*.

https://blogs.scientificamerican.com/observations/why-the-most-important-idea-in-behavioral-decision-making-is-a-fallacy/

Gambill, T. (2021, August 4). *The Art Of Asking Higher-Quality Questions*. Forbes.com.

https://www.forbes.com/sites/tonygambill/2021/08/04/the-art-of-asking-higher-quality-questions/?sh=129d31175592#relationalintelligence

Gartner. (2018). *Gartner Sales & Marketing Conference.*

Google. (2015, November 17). *The five keys to a successful Google team.* https://rework.withgoogle.com/. https://rework.withgoogle.com/blog/five-keys-to-a-successful-google-team/

Grant, A. (2020). *LinkedIn.* LinkedIn Post. https://www.linkedin.com/posts/adammgrant_if-you-define-success-solely-in-terms-of-activity-6692817979035447296-YYML/

Gregersen, H. B. (Harper Collins). *Questions Are The Answer.* 2018.

Guptara, J. (2020). *Business Storytelling: From Hype to Hack* (Kindle ed.). Pippa Ran Books & Media.

Hall, K. (2019). *Stories That Stick: How Storytelling Can Captivate Customers, Influence Audiences, and Transform Your Business.* HarperCollins Leadership.

Kendall, L. (2017). *Ninja Selling.* Greenleaf Book Group Press.

Khalsa, G. (n.d.). *Conscious Selling.* Conscious Selling. https://www.consciousselling.com/

Lawford. (2008, June 25). *Reagan-Mondale debate: the age issue.* YouTube.com. https://www.youtube.com/watch?v=LoPu1UIBkBc

Lee, B. (2013, August 14). *Bruce Lee Be As Water My Friend.* YouTube. https://www.youtube.com/watch?v=cJMwBwFj5nQ

Lunæros Studios. (2017, February 10). *Horshack Ooh Ooh.* YouTube. Retrieved July 2, 2021, from https://www.youtube.com/watch?v=ju-lptJweTc

Mandela, N. (2018, July 21). *17 Wise Nelson Mandela Quotes That Will Inspire Your Success*. INC.com. https://www.inc.com/peter-economy/17-wise-nelson-mandela-quotes-that-will-inspire-your-success.html#:~:text=%22May%20your%20choices%20reflect%20your,seems%20impossible%20until%20it's%20done.%22

Martini, N. (1998). *Customer-Focused Selling: Understanding customer needs, building trust, and delivering solutions...the smarter path to sales success*. Streetwise.

Merriam-Webster. (n.d.). *Dictionary by Merriam-Webster*. https://www.merriam-webster.com/. https://www.merriam-webster.com/dictionary/objection

Miller, D. (2017). *Building a StoryBrand: Clarify Your Message So Customers Will Listen*. HarperCollins Leadership.

Miller, W. (2012). *ProActive Selling: Control the Process--Win the Sale*. Amacom.

Morin, C., & Renvoise, P. (2018). *The Persuasion Code: How Neuromarketing Can Help You Persuade Anyone, Anywhere, Anytime*. Wiley.

Organizational Life Cycle. (2020, July 21). INC.com. https://www.inc.com/encyclopedia/organizational-life-cycle.html#:~:text=Five%20growth%20stages%20are%20observable,proceeds%20through%20the%20growth%20stages.

Pink, D. (2018). *When: The Scientific Secrets of Perfect Timing*. Canongate Books.

Schafer, J., & Karlins, M. (2015). *The Like Switch: An Ex-FBI Agent's Guide to Influencing, Attracting, and Winning People Over*. Atria Books.

Segal, P. (Director). (1995). *Tommy Boy* [Film]. Broadway Pictures.

Sinek, S. (2011). *Start with Why: How Great Leaders Inspire Everyone to Take Action*. Portfolio.

Voss, C., & Ross, T. (2017). *Never Split the Difference: Negotiating As If Your Life Depended On It*. Harper Business.

Zemeckis, R. (Director). (1985). *Back to the Future* [Film]. Universal Pictures.

Ziglar, Z. (1985). *Zig Ziglar's Secrets of Closing the Sale: For Anyone Who Must Get Others to Say Yes!* Berkley.

Made in United States
North Haven, CT
04 January 2024